For every problem,
there is a reason . . .
For every person,
there is a season . . .

To the little guys,
Tayo and Ravi.

ACKNOWLEDGMENTS

To Lindy Hess, our caring editor, who gave us the gift of her input, enthusiasm, and creativity, always championing our work and willing to stand up unflinchingly to support what she believes in. To Jane Rotrosen Berkey, agent extraordinaire, who makes truth and realism her friends and yet is open to finding the crack in the cosmic egg. To Samuel Vaughan, the Publisher of Doubleday, who gave our newest baby (this book) its wonderful and sensitive name.

To Ellen Kanner, who cared and dared enough to help plant the seeds from this book in many other gardens.

To Bruce, who loved us in a most special way; he challenged all of our unhappiness and helped us change our lives by asking the simplest, most disarming questions . . . without expectations or judgments.

To Sam Millen, who reaffirmed through his love and wanting that each of us has the power to change the world around us. To the members of the Millen family, who touched each other in ways never anticipated, demonstrating that grief and despair are not inevitable.

To our own mothers, Bertha and Ruth, who slipped by us before we, ourselves, knew how to talk with them during their times of transition. . . . finally, we have found a better way.

Prologue ৵৵৵৵৵৵৵৵৵৵৵৵৵

She touched us as best she could, often with great tenderness. Her arms held us close, fondled us, protected us from the real risks as well as the imaginary ones. Though the world changed unpredictably around us, she remained consistent; we knew, in the end, she would always be there for us. We called her "Mom" or "Mama" and, at times, when we became disgruntled, we addressed her as "Mother." Although, on occasion, she may have become embroiled in her own problems or acted in a manner distinctly less-than-perfect, most of us never doubted the underlying permanence and security in our relationship with her. All the words we had enshrined—family, home, security, love, acceptance—revolved around her presence. During those early years we never considered that her life could end, that the universe might rob from us the only person who accepted us without reservations despite the ripples on the surface. She didn't always have to understand us; she just had to be there.

Sam Millen, seventeen, and his family, faced what every family has or will confront eventually. Mama was dying and no one, least of all Sammy, had been prepared. His journey initiates dramatic changes in one American family's confrontation with death. What makes his story so special is his passion and daring to break the traditional pattern of denial and painful silence; in doing so, he becomes a teacher for each member of his family, forcing them, sometimes explosively, to face themselves and their fears, ultimately finding a new way to touch and love one another. But first Sammy had to stop his own retreat.

Most significantly, he breaks through the chain of pantomimed smiles and lies of reassurance in order to reach out to the woman who, in sickness, had been denied the humanity she once lavished on those around her.

This book will be an intimate, revealing, and hopeful portrait of real people facing a seemingly intolerable crisis. It will explore a mother's dying through the perspective of the father, the son, the daughter, grandparents, and friends. Despite the apparently devastating implications of the subject, *A Land Beyond Tears* tells the story of people who learn to go beyond the pain and discover new insights, joy, and even laughter. They find a new and special way to celebrate life, which becomes an inspiration for all of us.

Somewhere in this family, each of us will find ourselves . . . we'll see the frailties, but rather than curse them, we might just discover a different and uplifting way to handle a normally impossible situation—and light a candle in our own lives like Sam Millen and his family lit a candle in theirs.

Sam and I ran together, talked together, and shared a vision together. But this is not my story as much as it's Sam's story. Our sessions, which, in turn, precipitated encounters with other members of his family, created a loving and safe place for this young man to reveal himself . . . a place in which he not only screamed, cried, and shed the burden of many fears, but also came to see and accept himself, discovering insights and power he never imagined himself capable of possessing. To call Sammy courageous would be to separate him from all of us, when, in fact, he's one of us.

My work with Sam as facilitator, teacher, Option mentor, and friend not only suggests the possibilities of a therapeutic relationship, but provides wonderful evidence that if just one member of a family becomes more loving, then the entire dynamics of that family changes irrevocably. Sammy learned, in some profound way, that by changing himself, he changed the world around him.

Barry Neil Kaufman
("Bears")
New York, January 1982

The names of characters, places, and some irrelevant details have been changed in order to respect the involved individuals' rights to privacy.

The sun baked her face, sizzling the perspiration on her fore-head and reddening the tip of her nose. Her fingers embraced the steering wheel of her convertible limply. She maneuvered the car to the curb directly in front of the main entrance of the huge, three-story building which stretched the length of the entire block. This brick and stone high school, built in the late 1930s, loomed like a fortress, cold and uninviting. Colorful drawings decorated the bottom panels of one classroom in counterpoint to the acres of empty glass panes. Lisa Millen released the clutch of the ancient Fiat, purposely stalling it in gear beneath a sign which indicated ''no parking.'' Somehow, today, especially today, it did not matter. Nothing mattered.

Black sunglasses hid her eyes; blond, windblown hair danced in front of her face. She stared at the familiar wood doors, their heavy brass hinges sealing them tightly together in the stone frame . . . a mausoleum for grades eight through twelve. Though frozen like a manikin in her seat, Lisa occasionally dragged heavily on the cigarette dangling from her mouth, oblivious to the ashes collecting in her lap.

Two students, each carrying several books, ambled past the parked automobile, obviously attracted to its occupant as well as the machinery.

"Hey, hey—nice pair of wheels," one boy remarked as he nodded his head admiringly.

His friend smiled as well, then paused on the sidewalk. "We're the official welcoming committee," he boasted, "me and my friend, here." He adjusted his collar and approached the car. His eyes focused on her blouse. Despite its loose fit, the soft velour material highlighted the stingy, yet alluring, curves of her upper torso. He leaned over the windshield in order to catch a glimpse of the rest of her body. Her long legs met with his immediate approval, especially her tight and well-formed thighs. He made a grumbling sound in his throat in an effort to stimulate eye contact, but received no response. "I understand," he said. "You're the shy type. I can fix that. All you need is one round with ol' hot lips here."

The first boy, now visibly embarrassed by his friend's commentary and unnerved by this young woman's unflinching pose, pushed his companion away from the car. They jostled and muttered to each other as they left. "Ol' hot lips" turned and shouted several more suggestive remarks, but nothing invaded Lisa's internal space. She had slipped behind an invisible veil, detached from her body, insulated and numb.

Lisa had dreamed about this morning for many months, rehearsing the words to herself, mouthing them in the mirror. Ironically, she had not been elected to come to the school; she had volunteered. "Why did I offer?" she muttered to herself. Nausea licked the back of her throat. Her father had expressed his willingness to go, as did Chuck, a neighbor and friend. Yet, despite her dread, the chore fell to her. She had always known that she would be the one to tell her brother Sammy. She knew two days ago, two weeks ago, even two years ago, long before she had anything to tell.

The car door opened easily, too easily. Lisa walked along the sidewalk hesitantly, then mounted the staircase with resistant legs. Her breathing became noticeably irregular. She held her hand on the door handle for several minutes. Faded conversations flooded her ears, old faces drifted before her . . . memories aged and slightly muddled since her graduation four years ago. Finally, she lurched forward and entered the building.

Though her jeans and general appearance were indistinguishable from the students in the hall, her fast-paced walk separated her rather conspicuously from the crowd. Her eyes scrambled across bulletin boards she had once helped decorate. Another century. Another lifetime. Lisa wanted to scream in the hallway, to tell everyone around her how fast this would all be gone.

The panels of photographs commanded her attention. The muscles in her legs and abdomen tightened, almost painfully, as she stopped abruptly. Her long fingers slid the sunglasses to the top of her head. Bloodshot eyes peered out at the panorama of smiling faces. One board had been marked 1977. The photograph of the ''Honor Art Squad'' showed a younger, chunkier, laughing Lisa, arm in arm with her classmates. She studied her face, momentarily admiring its innocence, then scanned the other images. So many names had been forgotten. Lisa squinted, as she did frequently with her own oil paintings, and blurred the old black and white prints until they were merely a collection of anonymous heads and bodies. You have to let go of the past, she thought, you just have to.

Several school secretaries looked up when Lisa entered the administration office. No one recognized her and only one person smiled before returning to the litter of paper on her desk. Lisa stepped up to the counter forcefully. Oh God, yes, she mused, everything's in place, the chairs, the desks, the old clock, the aging map of North America, and the chipped bust of Daniel Webster.

''Excuse me,'' Lisa called to the woman seated closest to the door. ''Is Mrs. Flannery here?''

''Honey, she left well over two years ago. Anything I can help you with?''

''Well, yes, I, I guess so.''

Several minutes later, the same woman ushered Lisa into the principal's office. An older man, dressed in a tweed suit, entered from another door. His somber expression seemed rehearsed.

"Here, please, sit down," he said in a hushed voice. When his newly arrived guest remained standing, he forced an awkward smile. His left eyelid twitched nervously. "Well, you can use this office as long as you need to. Just take your time."

"No, ah, really, no thank you. I'd rather wait outside. Tell him I'll be outside, by the main entrance—okay?"

Both the principal and school secretary nodded as she exited.

Her body shivered in response to the wind as she sat on the stone stairs with her back to the doors of the school building. Her tall figure draped over several steps. Popping another cigarette into her mouth, Lisa ignited it expertly while gazing into the park across the street. A group of boys in blue and orange uniforms played hockey under the supervision of two coaches. An airborne volleyball bounced off the head of a short, heavy girl and flew over the net menacingly. Several people played racket ball against huge walls designed expressly for that purpose. Everything seemed in its natural order—so steady, so unshakable. These people had replaced the ones she once knew, part of an endless cycle which confused her. Though she had spent four years of her life in this school, at this moment it was as if she had never existed. Was death the same? she wondered . . . your chair, your bed, your clothes ultimately filled by other people, leaving your life and loves locked in the memory of a few, who, one day, might also forget.

The door opened behind her, but she did not turn around. Instead, Lisa held her breath, keeping her eyes focused on the activity across the street. Sam stared at his sister's back, holding his large hand over his mouth. Almost six feet tall, his lanky, athletic form suggested the presence of a person much older than sixteen. His forehead furrowed just above the bridge of his nose making his face appear prematurely lined. The corners of his eyes sloped downward and accented his already pensive gaze. Sam touched Lisa's shoulder firmly, but withdrew his hand quickly when she did not respond.

"Lise?" he said, fully aware of her identity.

4

She rose slowly, ignoring the tremor in her legs. The tears rolled down her cheeks to her own amazement. Despite the rehearsals, she had lost control.

"What?" Sam asked urgently, denying his own awareness.

When Lisa tried to talk, no words came. She put her arm around her brother and walked with him down the steps.

"Tell me," he pleaded.

Drawing in a deep breath, she blurted out a garbled sentence with only one very clear word—"died."

"Who died? Grandma?"

Lisa shook her head as she bit her bottom lip. Very clearly, in a low and penetrating voice, she said, "Mommy. Not Grandma. Mommy died."

Sam gaped at his sister wide-eyed. Adrenalin flooded his system, tripling the rate of his heartbeat instantly and lathering his skin with cold sweat. He pushed away from her, throwing his arms out over his head and twisting his body awkwardly as if responding to some internal eruption. Suddenly, his legs lunged forward, carrying him in a full sprint across the lawn and into the street.

"Sammy, Sammy," Lisa shouted, running after him.

When he reached the park, he ran onto a cinder track, slipping at first on the leather soles of his shoes. Rebalancing himself, he plunged forward like a horse charging out of the starter's gate. His long legs, which seemed to dangle when he walked, stretched in long, controlled strides. After the first quarter mile, he gained more speed, obviously moving faster and faster. His eyes appeared vacant; his movement hypnotic and studied.

Sitting on the empty bleachers, Lisa watched her brother, wanting to help, to comfort him, to be there and share the pain. But, like her, he had his own private way to absorb it, to integrate what they had all silently anticipated.

One of Sam's friends separated from the hockey team, apparently at the request of the coach, and jogged toward the track in search of an explanation for Sam's unauthorized appearance during what would normally be his third period English class.

"Sam, what are you doing here?" Brian shouted. "Everett's having a fit. Sam!" When he noticed Lisa, he slowed his pace, then stopped finally. Brian stared at her, suddenly understanding. He kicked the ground and turned, knowing not to intrude.

Sam pushed himself at full speed even after completing the second mile. For him, track had been more than a sport; it gave him a way to find a certain energy level within, a surge akin to meditation. His arms reached forward; his fingertips gripping the air in an effort to propel his body at greater speeds. Not once did he look at his sister. Not once did he break his concentration. After three miles at this frenzied pace, he lost his momentum, having run himself out. Nevertheless, he continued, pursuing the face of his mother; hearing their last conversation repeated; knowing all the words had ended; aware he had said good-bye but wanting another chance . . . just one more minute, ten more seconds to tell her that he loved her and would remember, would always remember.

Winded and drained, he dropped to the ground beside the track and rolled over onto his back. Beads of sweat bubbled on the surface of his face. His chest heaved, his body pulsating to the rhythm of his breathing.

Lisa knelt beside him, then sat down and lifted his head into her lap. Her fingers slid over his wet forehead and through his hair. She had never felt so loving toward him, so affectionate, so caring . . . so motherly.

He glared up at the clouds. "Funny," he said, his voice thin and cracking, "this was her favorite kind of day—those big cotton candy clouds hanging so low. How come she died on her favorite day?"

Lisa hugged him. "Sammy, let go. If you want to cry . . . cry!"

"Do we have to go back now?" he asked, ignoring her statement.

"When you're ready, we'll go home."

"Is she still there . . . in the house?"

"No, Sammy, I think she's gone."

He rose to his feet, then helped his sister up. They walked hand in hand across the field. Sam hummed the melody from the *Peer Gynt Suite,* a symphony his mother adored. He envisioned her lying in her bed, her eyes closed, a half-smile on her face as music filled her bedroom. Turning to his sister, he said, "Lisa, can I hug you?"

She nodded and held him tightly, feeling his body convulse as he cried.

Margaret Millen's passing had been expected. Her son Sam, her daughter Lisa, and her husband Chad had prepared for this moment, almost invited it. When Sam cried in his sister's arms, he could feel himself letting go, releasing his mother this final time.

For many who knew Margaret, the process of grieving had begun long before her death. Most had come to the funeral to witness the last dignified chapter. A familiar ritual. Tears. Sobbing. That peculiar hushed quiet between prayers. Everything in its place . . . at least almost everything. Some friends of the family noticed the peculiarity immediately. Others tried to ignore it. The pastor assumed Chad, Lisa, and Sam were still in shock. The druggist, who often attended the funerals of his best customers, decided without hesitation that this poor woman must have died unloved. Everyone had come to share the pain, but the process had been short-circuited by the calm, peaceful expressions and fleeting smiles which rippled across the faces of Margaret Millen's children and husband.

Sam had left a note at my home, asking me to attend. I'm not big on funerals, although I certainly understand their function. When I entered the chapel through a side door, Samuel Millen waved vigorously and shouted "Bears!" I couldn't help but smile broadly, despite the quizzical and disapproving glances of some parishioners. My joy at seeing this young man's bright eyes had not been intended as a statement of disrespect. I remembered my own mother's funeral and my own personal demonstration of pain at that time. How little I understood or

7

knew then. My journey toward trusting myself and expressing love began long after her death, while Sam's journey began before his mother's passing.

Charles Millen, Sam's grandfather, nodded in my direction, then winked cheerfully at the crucifix suspended behind the pulpit. Ol' Charlie made friends with most everyone, man or God. He had said good-bye to his daughter-in-law while she was alive and therefore had little interest in this solemn ceremony. His eyes danced in their sockets as he studied his son and two grandchildren, obviously delighted in their apparent comfort. Everyone had come to mourn, except these four people.

Before the service began, Sam left his place, crossed the center aisle, and approached me as I stood against a side wall of the church. He embraced me robustly. "That's from my mom," he said, ". . . really!" We stared at each other for several seconds. I don't remember who smiled first, but, suddenly, we both laughed. Sam's eyes became glazed. "Thanks, Bears," he said as he backed away and rejoined his father and sister.

Sam asked that I begin his story here, so others could know that he loved his mother with an easy smile and some laughter on the day of her funeral. He wanted everyone to remember the end of his struggle and the gift of finding a loving way to say good-bye.

No one in the Millen family, not even Sam, could have predicted what happened in those final weeks before Margaret's death. In order to share with you the flowering of a young man who dared to challenge himself and a course of agony that most families believe they have to endure, I must go back further than those last few weeks—five months to be exact.

2 ᘐᘐᘐᘐᘐᘐᘐᘐᘐᘐᘐᘐᘐᘐᘐᘐᘐᘐᘐᘐᘐ

The exposed, massive, steel superstructure of the building loomed like a prehistoric dinosaur over the art and sculpture it housed. Sam stared at the unmasked bolts and rivets, intrigued by the cluster of lights sparkling like diamonds in the center of the room. A naked building with ornaments, he quipped to himself. That image immediately triggered an old, yet vivid, imprint that he recalled easily from a peeping-Tom expedition he once participated in at twelve years old. He had climbed on the shoulders of a friend and peered through the window of a neighbor's house. To his incredulous surprise, he saw a woman completely naked with jewelry glittering from around her neck and wrists. When she almost backed into the window with her more-than-ample buttocks, Sam gasped at the large bulbous forms with their soft dimples. Instinctively, he pushed away from the building, throwing both himself and his friend off balance. His face flushed as he remembered the incident. Sam looked around self-consciously. An elegantly attired woman, wearing a satin dress that stretched over her body like a glove, eyed him with obvious amusement. Feeling transparent, Sam turned away abruptly and disappeared into the crowd.

The work of six university students had been highlighted in the gallery's latest show. Their paintings ranged from personal statements to abstract exercises in form and color. One artist had, in fact, designed his pieces as extensions of mathematical equations. Sam stared at the simple rectangular panels of color and squinted as he had seen his sister do often. She had told him to look for the inner painting, which he now tried to extract optically without much success. Moving away from the wall, he wedged a path through the crowd, fixing on various faces and listening to fragments of conversations.

"Genuinely moving, my dear," an older woman swooned. She pointed authoritatively at one painting, a gesture which matched her Queen Victorian dress. "The subtleties of line entrapping space, the exquisite patterns of light . . ."

"They don't have art shows anymore," argued a suited man to the group gathered around him, "just variations on outer space."

Another man scrutinized his paper cup suspiciously. He dipped his index finger into the liquid and then touched it to his tongue. "The apple cider stinks," he declared.

A girl in jeans whispered to a friend, "I think he's sexy, right down to his big toe."

Sam smiled at her, but she ignored him. Instead of her face being an invitation, it became a barrier, an armored mask sculptured with two eyes, a nose, and a mouth. Faces. On the outside, there's only faces, he told himself. Maybe there's an inner person like an inner painting. Cupping his hand around his left eye, Sam scanned the crowd as if peering through a camera lens: a bald head, lipstick mouths, painted eyelids, red fingernails, white gloves. He wondered whether he, too, had his camouflage as his fingers tugged instinctively on the collar of his white shirt, suddenly upset at being straitjacketed in a suit and tie.

The harsh purples and garish maroons of distorted circus figures along the north wall drew his attention. Sam stared at the clown's face. The lips drooped down on one side and the forehead stretched upward on the other. Sam knew he didn't have to squint to see the inner painting this time. He pushed his own lips downward, then raised his eyebrows mimicking the expression in the painting.

At that instant, a handsome woman in tailored clothes came up behind him and poked him playfully in the ribs. Startled, Sam whipped around.

"Oh, Mom."

Margaret Millen took her son's arm proudly. "How about you and I spending a little more time admiring your sister's paintings." Sam nodded his consent as his mother directed him through the crowd.

At thirty-nine, Margaret Millen moved quietly and, until recently, happily, into her middle years. Only in the past few months had her face betrayed evidence of the aging process. Small lines creased the skin at the corners of her eyes and edged a soft smile around her mouth. But her sandy-colored hair, turned under at shoulder length, and her trim figure still gave Margaret the appearance of a woman ten years her junior. She delighted in the fact that Sam often introduced her as his older sister.

As she approached the west wall with her son, she couldn't help but smile at the sign which identified the artist whose works were exhibited in this section—"LISA MILLEN." These paintings differed dramatically from the others in the show. Lisa's portraits had a distinct photographic quality with soft edges and muted colors. Most of them depicted gentle and distinctly personal exchanges between two or three women in either an urban or rural landscape. One reviewer had compared them with European folk art of the eighteenth century. Another labeled them political in content, suggesting that they articulated themes evident in the women's movement.

Margaret pointed to one of the paintings.

"What do you think?"

Sam cocked his head to the side. "It's okay."

"Just okay?" she asked.

He glanced at her cautiously, then crossed his arms rather pompously, leaned his chin into his hand and puckered his lips. Satisfied with the authenticity of an art critic's pose, he cleared his throat and spoke in an unusually deep voice.

"The subtleties of line, uh, entrapping space." A self-conscious smile broke the sanctity of his performance. "I like it," he said. "I like it a lot."

Margaret kissed him lightly and squeezed his arm.

"Me too," She admired the painting again. "Your sister's a very gentle soul." A pause. "And so are you, Sam."

Three people moved directly in front of Margaret and Sam.

"Now what do you suppose these are all about?" one man barked. He slipped his hands into his pockets and sighed.

"Henry, you always see everything with your left brain. You don't analyze art, you experience it." The woman jerked her head backward. Her eyes narrowed as she squinted studiously at the painting. Both Sam and his mother watched her expression relax into a satisfied smile.

"They should say something," the other man said impatiently.

"But they do!" Margaret blurted.

The three people turned toward her, surprised by the interruption. An awkward moment of silence. The heat in Margaret's face signaled to her that she had blushed, but she recovered from her initial embarrassment within seconds.

"I agree with you," the other woman said. "They're lyrical."

"Yes, yes," Margaret concurred. She moved closer to the trio. "And they're daring . . . because, because they're human. Look at everything around us," she continued, "mechanical, cold, but not these paintings, oh no, not these."

"She's right, Henry. I'd like to buy this one."

"Are you kidding?" the man asked.

"It's a steal," Margaret interjected. "Really, a steal." She knew she could do it, just this once; sell it to them, make them love it like she did. That's what she needed, she thought, a crusade—her daughter's paintings, the children she once worked with at St. Dominick's, Sam's track competition—almost anything would do. She couldn't let herself slide any further. Instinctively, she grabbed her son's hand tightly, too tightly. When he glanced at her, Margaret Millen smothered her inner dialogue, quickly continuing the show for both herself and her son. She mimicked Sam's previous impersonation of an art critic, then winked at him as he suppressed a giggle and withdrew.

As Sam backed away, he watched his mother engage the other woman again. She had made it seem so easy. He cursed his self-consciousness, then shuffled his feet across the floor, tracking an imaginary line near the wall. When he rounded the far corner, he noticed his father talking to an older man sporting a Salvador Dali moustache. Sam circled behind them and listened to their conversation.

"The exposure is uplifting, truly," Professor Kingly insisted, "for the students as well as the school." He paused to give his words the proper respect. If he didn't take himself seriously, who would?

Chad Millen considered Kingly to be a pompous ass, but he could handle him. "This is quite an honor for Lisa," he said. "She takes her art quite seriously."

"And so she should!" Kingly declared. "Your daughter has that special spark . . . maybe one in a thousand have it, maybe one in ten thousand. Very, very delicate. Almost fragile. She has to be nurtured, supported."

Chad nodded and displayed one of those mechanical smiles he usually reserved for his business clients.

"And that's what we do here," the professor continued. "That's what I do, Mr. Millen."

"I know. Lisa admires you very much, Professor Kingly," Chad said. Finally, it was done. He had done his share with this sanctimonious instructor. No one could ever accuse him of sabotaging his daughter's career. No one.

When the professor began speaking again, Chad no longer listened. Margaret occupied his thoughts as he watched her animated form across the room.

"You see, I don't want admiration," Kingly added. "I want dedication, hard work! Applied art means just that . . . applying one's self."

Chad smiled as he noticed his wife laugh.

13

"I knew you'd agree with me," the professor said, tapping Millen's arm almost affectionately.

Lisa stood at another end of the room, engaged in a group discussion with some friends. As the conversation ebbed, her eyes surveyed the noisy clutter of people in the gallery. She saw her father with Professor Kingly, then noticed her brother lurking in the crowd behind them. Excusing herself, she disengaged from her friends and cornered Sam.

"Are you playing wallflower or superspy?" she whispered.

"Neither," Sam said matter-of-factly.

"Just eavesdropping, huh?"

Lisa knew she had hit the mark when her brother smiled.

"You can relax, you know. I'm not going to ask you what you think of my work, okay?"

"But I think your stuff is neat," he protested.

Suddenly, Jessica, Lisa's friend, strutted between them. "Sorry to interrupt the love affair, but your sister and I have some business to discuss."

"Can't it wait? Sam and I . . ."

"Come, come—your family had you for the last twenty-one years; now it's my turn. Ta-ta." She flashed a smug grin at Sam, then whisked his sister off into the crowd.

Sam watched them leave, expecting Lisa to turn around, just once—but she didn't. He blamed Jessica. She's a turkey, he told himself, and you don't blow yourself away on turkeys.

Margaret, now alone, smiled as she perused the remainder of her daughter's paintings. She cocked her head at one, confronting it and admiring it at the same time. The delicate depiction of an embrace between an older and younger woman reminded her of her own childhood, when people expressed their affection more easily and more openly. Had she given to her own children what her mother had lavished upon her? Or, had she been discreet, like her neighbors, bypassing physical contact for more verbal expressions of caring? With some children, like those she had helped at St. Dominick's, the needs had been apparent. Starved, maimed, deformed, handicapped—little people abandoned by a culture uncomfortable with its own imperfections. But what about those who seemed whole on the outside? Like Lisa or Sam or Chad or, even, her? Everyone wants to be touched, Margaret thought. Was that Lisa's message to her and to the world in these paintings? She promised herself to hug her daughter the very next time she saw her.

Moving on, Margaret stared at another of Lisa's paintings, which was being scrutinized simultaneously by two other women.

"Does everyone have to air their dirty laundry in public these days?" With a gallant flick of her arm, the woman gestured toward all the companion portraits. "Very lesbian material, if you ask me."

"Don't be so prissy," the other woman countered.

Margaret gaped at these two ladies. What an outrageous observation, she thought. Lisa? She looked back at her daughter's paintings, suddenly seeing them from an entirely different perspective.

"She flaunts it," the first woman added. "You don't have to be a psychiatrist to see that. Not a man in sight; just women touching women—how cute!"

It never had occurred to her, but, indeed, not a single male image could be found in any of her daughter's paintings. As Margaret turned around, she winced, almost imperceptibly. A chair, a bench, anything . . . she knew she had to find a place to sit down. Her hands pressed against her upper abdomen as she hunched over in pain.

Excusing himself in mid-conversation with Professor Kingly, Chad moved quickly through two groups of people. Not once had he allowed his wife to drift beyond his point of vision. From the other side of the room, Sam also spotted his mother's difficulty. At first his legs seemed frozen, but, finally, he began to push his way through the crowd.

Chad swept in from behind and supported Margaret from around her waist.

"How's my girl doing?"

Straightening herself with great effort, she said, "Oh, I'm okay. It's just the medication acting up in my poor belly."

Sam approached cautiously.

"That's what I like to hear, Maggie," Chad said. "Just hang in there. You'll be fine."

"That's right, Mom," Sam added, taking his father's cue. "Mind over matter."

If Margaret couldn't force a smile for her husband, she certainly managed one for her son.

"A lady in distress sure gets a lot of attention from you fellows."

"I'll get the coats," Sam said.

Within seconds, he had crossed the room, thankful for the chore. As he approached the coatroom, the voice of his sister stopped him.

"Hey, Sam," Lisa called, walking briskly toward him with Jessica on her arm. "Are you leaving?"

"Mom's tired," Sam said, purposely avoiding her eyes. "I'm getting our coats." When he took a step forward, Lisa touched his arm softly.

"Anything wrong? The party's only begun."

"I said she's just tired," he answered abruptly.

"I hear you," Lisa replied.

"I'm sorry. I guess I'm tired too."

"Mom's a bit anemic," Lisa said, addressing her friend. "Let me say good-bye, okay?" Jessica shrugged.

"They're over there," Sam said, pointing.

As Lisa approached her parents, they rose from the bench Chad had located.

"Sam says you're going. You okay, Mom?"

Chad smiled. "Your mother's fine."

"I'm so proud of you, honey," Margaret said. "You're a fine artist." She had forgotten about her resolution to hug her daughter.

Lisa nodded appreciatively to her mother. "And you, Dad. How do you like my paintings?"

16

"Well, your professor seems to think you really have what it takes."

"But what do *you* think?"

"I'm an engineer, Lisa, not an art critic."

Sam arrived with the coats bundled between his arms. Immediately, he helped his mother into hers.

"The rock," Chad said, tapping his fist on his son's shoulder approvingly. "You're a good boy, Sam."

His cheeks dropped down past the bottom of his jawline like an ancient Basset hound; the folds of skin over his eyes looked more like umbrellas than eyelids. And yet, despite the seventy-four years of erosion which ravaged Charles Millen's face, his mouth betrayed an almost impish grin as he leaned over the handlebars, allowing the bicycle to coast into a curve. Then, with sudden determination, he pumped the pedals, dipping his chin into his chest in order to minimize the wind resistance. For a moment, the old man became a jockey leading his mount into the final stretch . . . only the track was macadam and the horse had two wheels.

The brakes began to squeal as he slowed the bike and withdrew one of the many folded newspapers from a side basket. Without stopping, he snapped his wrist rather professionally, sending the paper up over a parked Jaguar and into a tree-lined driveway. Charlie repeated this process as he passed most of the houses.

In the seclusion of the garage, Sam paused from sweeping and leaned on the broom. The bizarre figure of his grandfather, riding Timothy Blackwell's bike, had caught his attention. Years ago, Charlie Millen, an oddity, a relic from an old photo album, had been a source of embarrassment for him. Even now, Sam had to make allowances. His grandfather wore a baseball hat turned backward on his head; the pant leg closest to the chain had been rolled up to his knee. Since he no longer permitted anyone to cut his hair, his thick gray curls danced wildly down his neck and over his ears. A brightly colored handkerchief had been tied loosely around his forehead; one end flapped in the wind. If Sam had been alone on an island, he could have cheered for his grandfather as he had done often as a toddler. Instead, he watched silently, wondering what made some people so different, never suspecting that his grandmother and father had already begun to label most of the old man's peculiarities as early signs of senility.

Chad, down on one knee, turned the soil expertly before laying the garden ruler on the ground. Every four inches, he wedged a hole with his shovel, set a tulip bulb into the ground, and buried it exactly three quarters of an inch beneath the surface. Margaret, working nearby, shaped the outer edge of a juniper, one of thirty which rimmed their suburban ranch house like a series of green doilies.

"The soil's perfect this year, Maggie. Remember that postcard Lisa sent us last year from Switzerland with all the beautiful-colored flowers; well, when these tulips come up, and the azaleas bloom, it's going to look like a Swiss wonderland right here."

Margaret smiled at her husband. She might have answered him, added to the imagery, but her energy had begun to drain. Nevertheless, Chad's rare use of metaphor did not go unnoticed.

The screeching sound of rubber against metal distracted both of them. As Chad and Margaret turned, Charlie Millen mimicked the bike's brakes by making a high-pitched squealing sound in his throat. He brought the bicycle to an abrupt halt and dismounted. He smiled at his son and daughter-in-law, adjusted the kick stand, then began a quick series of jumping jacks.

"One-two, one-two, one-two."

Margaret removed her gardening gloves and squatted on the ground, intrigued and delighted by the old man's burst of energy. Chad stood up and placed his hands on his hips. The opening between his eyelids narrowed as he watched his father.

Charlie's animated form came to a quick rest, but only for a second or two. He proceeded immediately to do a set of deep-knee bends; then, after placing his hands on his head, he lifted his legs high and circled his two-wheeled vehicle like a prancing palomino.

Margaret giggled, putting her hand instinctively over her mouth. The old man's antics reminded her of the wide-eyed, uninhibited behavior she had witnessed so often in children . . . and Margaret Millen loved children.

"Are you in training for something, Pop?" Chad asked flatly.

"Nope," Charlie answered cheerfully. "Just keeping in shape for my newspaper route."

Chad's mother, Myrna, a chunky woman in her mid-sixties, pushed the front door aside and stood in the archway holding a wooden spoon. The sight of her husband beside the bike made her wince. She sighed, then folded her arms in front of her.

"Since when do you have a paper route?" Chad pressed.

"Since I'm helping Timothy Blackwell down the street."

"Pop, the Blackwell kid doesn't need your help. He's a healthy fourteen-year-old and you're seventy-four years old."

Charlie laughed as he initiated a final set of deep-knee bends. "Well, today . . . he feels seventy-four and I feel fourteen—so I'm taking over!" The old man slapped his leg and cackled merrily.

Margaret began to laugh. Chad shook his head disapprovingly. He disliked what he could not control. Somehow, almost imperceptively, their roles had reversed. He had become the scolding father, while Charlie behaved like a rebellious adolescent, unwilling to confine himself to what others deemed proper etiquette. Chad wanted to be more patient. When he repeated the word senility to himself and thought of clogged arteries and brain cells deprived of oxygen, he eased off his father's case. That was an "engineering" problem he could readily understand. And yet, despite what he envisioned as inevitable plumbing problems in the human system, he had the distinct sensation that his father made clear choices to behave as he did; at those times, Chad found it difficult to accept his father's routines.

When the old man noticed his wife at the door, he seized the frisbee from the front basket of the bike and said, "Hey, Myrna, here, catch!"

Grinning from ear to ear, Charlie threw the frisbee to his wife. Just as it reached her, she slammed it down with her wooden spoon.

"Now, Charles Millen, you just stop acting like a damn fool . . ."

"It's okay, Mom," Maggie said quietly. "He's just having a good time."

"Aah!" Myrna muttered. "Good time, my foot. Half the things he does, he does just to annoy me." She turned angrily and disappeared back into the house. For her, the word senility was just another curse of advancing age; it meant that her husband would now do more freely those unruly kinds of behavior that he previously had the good sense to suppress.

The man has a great arm, Sam thought, admiring his grandfather's accuracy with the frisbee despite the distance between them. He had watched the exchange for several minutes, finally entering the front yard cautiously. He stood next to his father as Charlie jumped onto his bicycle. The old man almost toppled it, but then rode off, one foot dangling haphazardly off its pedal. Sam started to cheer, but stopped short and adopted a serious pose upon observing Chad's stern expression.

"The man's going to kill himself," Chad muttered.

"At least he'll have a real good time before he goes," Margaret commented as she climbed slowly to her feet and walked in the direction of the house. Suddenly, overcome by a dizzy spell, she fell backward uncontrollably and groaned. Chad and Sam whirled around as Margaret collapsed on the lawn.

"Maggie," Chad shouted, reaching out his arms as if to, somehow, magically soften her fall, but the twenty feet separating them robbed him of that possibility.

"Mom," Sam whispered weakly as his father's arms lunged past his head.

They both ran toward her. Chad knelt down and slipped his hand beneath her. "Help me to get her to the chaise."

Margaret moaned as her husband and son carried her.

"It's okay, sweetheart. Really! We're just going to lay you down so you're comfortable."

With studious care, they eased her gently onto the chaise. The color had drained from her face. She reached for her husband's hand, squeezing it tightly in an attempt to neutralize the spinning inside her head.

"Sam, go get a glass of water."

A glass of water. A glass of water. His father's words echoed in his ears as he lurched forward and ran into the house.

"You're okay, Maggie," Chad said quietly, almost too quietly. "Just one of those little dizzy spells. The doctor warned us, remember?" She nodded. "A dizzy spell," he said, "That's all, you hear, that's all."

Sam charged through the door, lunged off the front steps, and delivered the water to his mother. Margaret forced a smile as her husband handed her one of the five vials sitting on the table next to the chaise. Sam noticed them before, many times before, but he never catalogued them or consciously reviewed their presence.

Chad turned to his son. "Don't look so frightened, Sammy. She's okay." He eyed his wife. "Right, you young chicken."

Margaret pushed out another smile.

"Oh, I know she's okay, Dad," Sam insisted. "I know. Probably just overdid it a little last night at the opening. That's all. I know." As he finished his last sentence, his eyes scanned the array of medicine again. The back of his throat tightened. Sam wanted to tell somebody he was scared. He wanted to stop growing up, to stop seeing, to stop questioning. Suddenly, he felt his father's firm grip on his shoulder. He met Chad's confident nod with a fabricated grin. Sam Millen refused to allow his body to betray any weakness. He had to be strong.

His leg vibrated, almost hypnotically, as he sat by his desk waiting for the bell to ring. Sam used to dream about becoming invisible, dematerializing and materializing at will. Mr. Chokker, his English teacher, pushed him back into this toddler fantasy as he read everyone's composition marks aloud. Sam knew what was coming. As the instructor called out Jeannie Lawrence's grade, he held his breath. He would be next. Sam slid slightly forward in his chair and crouched over his desk.

"Millen. A C-minus. And that's after giving you the benefit of the doubt, young man. Too much daydreaming. Not enough work, Sammy-boy." Several students turned their heads and smiled.

Now, Sam thought to himself, one, two, three, disappear. He stared at his legs, noting his body riveted to the seat and very visible to everyone in the class. He didn't need Mr. Chokker to make a public announcement in order for him to know his ability to concentrate had declined.

"Too much sex, eh, Sammy-boy," Josh Jenkins whispered to him across the aisle.

"Guess so," Sam lied.

He darted out of the class first as soon as the bell rang. Sam felt more comfortable in movement than at rest. His long legs propelled him down two flights of stairs. He turned the knob to the locker room door and entered briskly. To his surprise, the benches were empty. They're still on the track, he thought. Must be running late. Sam Millen turned the combination on his lock. Despite the fact that he had done it a thousand times before, he kept missing the numbers.

"Shit!" he muttered. He consulted his watch, anxious to finish before the team returned. Finally, the last flip hit the mark and the base of the lock dropped two full inches. Sam opened the door and deposited his books on the top shelf. He tried to ignore the clippings and photographs taped to the inside walls. One print, plastered on the front of the school newspaper, depicted him with his arms up as he ran across the finish line at full speed. A five-word headline dwarfed all the other news on the page. "Millen Leads at Rockland High."

The door slamming shut sounded like an explosion as the noise ricocheted off the walls of metal closets. Sam jiggled the lock closed and then paused, listening to the rumble of sneakered feet sprinting through the corridor. He considered waiting, but, then, almost instinctively, darted out the door and up the staircase.

The school lunchroom presented its usual atmosphere of chaos. A voluptuous girl, smiling through gobs of lip gloss, dropped her books casually before a table of male admirers, who, in turn, scurried to retrieve her property. Another teenager whined as her classmates tossed her pocketbook from table to table. After shimmying up a pole, an athletic young man yelled from the top, "I'm going to fly!" An assortment of greetings and obscenities catapulted back and forth across the room like mortar fire.

Seated at a crowded table near the far wall, Sam attempted to involve himself in an ongoing conversation without much success. He chomped on a tunafish sandwich mechanically. The light-headedness, which had panicked him earlier in the morning, continued to plague him. Maybe I'm getting sick, Sam thought as he fought the wave of nausea washing over him. As discreetly as possible, he removed the half-chewed piece of sandwich from his mouth and wrapped it quickly in a napkin. No one had noticed. A smile of relief blossomed momentarily, then faded as Sam sensed a peculiar kind of weightlessness, as if his body had become buoyant, floating just fractions of an inch off the chair. Had this been the sensation his mother had just before she fainted? Bracing himself against the table, Sam waited. He tried to imagine what it would feel like to see the lights dim, his classmates blur, and the lunchroom fade into complete darkness. Perspiration oozed from the palms of his hands, diminishing the firmness of his grip on the metal table. Sam remained frozen, hanging on. A long minute passed. No darkened room. No blurred vision. He glanced down at his hands. The blood had drained from them so completely that the color beneath his fingernails had faded to a milky white. Sam relaxed his hands and sighed. He couldn't afford to get sick, not now. His family needed him at home. The rock. He called me the rock, Sam remembered, and here I am, sweaty palms and all. Loud laughter intercepted the flow of his thoughts.

Bud, a short boy with greasy hair and a runaway case of acne, joked, "Mr. Petrucci said in twenty years of teaching, he's never had any kid that's been as big a headache as Hank."

Hank sat next to him, sporting a cowboy hat which also made him appear even taller than his six-foot height. He slumped into his chair, tipping it back onto two legs, and had one foot draped across the top of the table. A toothpick dented his bottom lip. He was a star in his own right. The two boys laughed boisterously.

Hank added, "Yeah! So I says, well, I guess I'm just one of those kids only a mother could love. And Mr. Petrucci says, 'Oh, it's not that I don't love you, Hank. It's just that I'm running out of aspirins.' "

He burst into a thunder of laughter, but stopped abruptly, noticing Sam, who was the only one at the table not joining in the festivities.

"Hey, you guys," he said, "ya know Sammy-boy's dropped out of the track team?"

Sam furrowed his forehead and stuffed the remains of his sandwich into his mouth, almost choking.

Hank continued. "Now if that would've happened with me on the football team, there wouldn't be no football team, right Bud?"

Bud gave his usual, "For sure, Hank," and the two of them continued their chorus of laughter.

Sam wanted to leave the table, but decided not to give Hank the satisfaction. He wondered why Hank's sick humor had such favorable responses.

He looked away and noticed a girl from his social studies class pass by. There was something about the way she glided across the floor that intrigued Sam. Her swanlike head movements were supported by the wispiness of her arms and legs; a ballet of extremities.

When Hank caught Sam looking at her, he said, "Watch this, Buddy-boy!" One side of Hank's mouth tilted up as his head betrayed a slight turn toward Ginny.

"Hey, Ginny, got anything good I can munch on? I'm still hungry."

Ginny looked at him innocently. "No, sorry."

Hank then replied, "That's okay, I'll just munch on you then."

Everyone roared except Sam and his friend Brian. Ginny gave Hank a disgusted glance and, with a flip of her head, glided away.

Brian peered at Sam, who shook his head. Don't say a word, he begged Brian silently. But Brian had seen enough. He looked down at his hand, which had a puppet face drawn on it, the thumb activating its mouth, and ventriloquized in a high, squeaky voice. "You know, Hank, you're real funny. Ha! Ha! Ha! And your face goes with your jokes; it's ugly."

In another voice, Brian continued, "And how ugly is that?"

Reverting to his original squeaky voice, he answered his

own question. ''He's so ugly that when you look up the word 'ugly' in the dictionary, there's a little picture of Hank's face there. Ha! Ha! Ha!''

Hank and Bud bolted from their chairs, grabbing Brian from across the table.

Sam intercepted immediately, saying, ''Hey, he was just joking, Hank. He's a big joker, like you. Right?'' He waited for their reactions and then added, ''Listen, I've got some great homemade cookies my mom baked. Here, try one.''

Hank whipped himself away. ''You crazy? Wouldn't eat any food from you!''

Bud agreed, adding, ''It might be catching.''

Sam looked puzzled. What do they mean, catching?

Ripping his jacket from the back of his chair, Hank spit his toothpick out, propelling it across the table toward Brian. ''C'mon, Bud,'' he said, ''let's get out of here before he contaminates us.''

Bud attempted a duplication of Hank's actions, but caught the zipper of his jacket on his V-neck sweater. He yanked it loose, tearing his sweater. The two boys pranced away in a cloud of their own snickers.

''What's going on with them? What do they mean, catching?'' Sam asked the others at the table.

A freckly-faced boy looked down and began doodling on his looseleaf. Another reached for the floor to retie his already tied sneaker.

''Who knows, Sam . . . and who cares anyway,'' said a third boy.

The first boy added hesitantly, ''Don't listen to them.''

Sam turned to face his friend. Brian sat quietly, staring into the puppet face drawn on his hand. He wished he could think of something funny for his puppet to say. Nothing came.

''Brian,'' Sam pushed, ''hey, tell me.'' Brian knew he couldn't lie to Sam. He owed it to him to be honest.

''It's, um . . . it's . . . your mom, Sam.''

''My mom?''

Brian nodded his head and continued. "You know, her being sick and everything . . ." Brian wished he'd stayed home today. "Hey, listen Sam, they're just a bunch of creeps . . ."

His voice trailed off as he watched Sam disappear from the lunchroom. Despite all the noise, Brian heard the doors to the yard slam shut.

Once outside, gusts of misty, cool air alleviated some of Sam's light-headedness. Each breath he drew in aided in the support of his faltering system. He leaned on the back of a bench and rested his head between his hands. He wanted to scream, but concluded that would only bring onlookers, curiosity-seekers.

Aware of a figure bolting from the school, Ginny watched Sam from a nearby bench. She considered approaching him to ask if she could help. But nobody wants to be bothered when they're having a rough day, she decided, at least not until they've had some time alone.

Dropping his arms, Sam lifted his head toward the sky, then scanned the area dotted with trees. He spotted Ginny. Pulling himself together, he smiled self-consciously, hoping she hadn't been watching him for long. She smiled back. Sam put his hands in his pockets, took a deep breath and walked leisurely toward Ginny. She closed her book and waited.

Sam pushed out an overly friendly "Hi."

Ginny returned the "hi" with a slight giggle.

"Hope you didn't let that clown throw you before," he said.

"No, not really," she replied.

"Well, I'd better head back," Sam said, glancing at his watch. "See ya." Slowly, he pivoted.

Ginny wanted to say more, but all she could get out was, "Um . . ."

Sam jerked around quickly. "What?"

Ginny almost kicked herself for not being able to come up with something even the slightest bit profound. She settled for an off-handed, "Well, uh . . . nothing."

"So . . . I'll see ya," Sam muttered, picking a dandelion and twirling it between his fingers as he backed away. Eventually, he turned and began whistling to the wind.

5 ♫ ♫ ♫ ♫ ♫ ♫ ♫ ♫ ♫ ♫ ♫ ♫ ♫ ♫ ♫ ♫ ♫ ♫ ♫

Chad Millen, impatient with the crosstown traffic, catapulted himself easily from the taxi and glided into a brisk walk down 56th Street. Shoulders back. Chin up. Hands swinging in a perfect cadence with the opposite foot. Chad prided himself on his posture and body tone. No expanding mid-section slopping over his belt buckle. No sagging pectoral muscles feminizing his chest. His waist had expanded less than two inches in twenty years. As he lifted his foot and hopped over the curb, the extension of his leg reminded him of leaping for a basket. I could do it again, he thought. I could. Thirty-eight points against Columbia; most of them in the second half. High scorer. His record stood unbeaten for six years. Every time he dunked another ball into the basket, the students jumped to their feet and screamed, "Go, Millen! Go!" Maybe that was the reason he loved to watch Sam compete. They shouted the same words to his son. "Go, Millen! Go!" Chad tried to visualize the faces of those sitting on the bleachers, but couldn't. He tried to hear the applause, but the years had muted the sounds of those memories.

"Pardon me, sir," the old woman intruded. "I'm collecting for the moms of the world." Her tattered clothing and two shopping bags filled with all her worldly possessions seemed

31

oddly out of place on restaurant row. Chad had not intended to stop, although he slowed his pace considerably.

"Sorry," he said softly, never looking directly at her.

The bag lady refused to be discouraged. She pursued him, holding her hand in front of his chest as he moved. "Just a dollar." A smile creased her pocked face. She attempted to flutter her eyelids unsuccessfully. "Okay, governor, how about fifty cents for an old lady?" Her fingers curled in anticipation.

"Jesus," Chad hissed. He extended his gait. The old lady began to trot. Several undergarments fell from one of her bags, but she didn't seem to notice. Chad did. He stopped abruptly and faced her; the anger edged around his eyes was apparent.

She persisted. "A quarter for some coffee. What's a quarter to the likes of you?"

He withdrew a pile of change from his pocket, located a quarter, and dropped it into her hand. She stared at the remaining coins, which he dumped back into his pants.

"You bastard," she said, "I know your kind."

Chad Millen peered at her coldly. The muscles along his jawbone flexed. Something in his eyes frightened the old lady, who turned quickly and scurried away.

"Lieutenant Millen, give her something," the soldier had begged him. Unlike an old basketball game, he remembered every detail of that incident.

"That's not the way you teach people," he had screamed back. "A land of beggars . . . is that what you guys want?" One soldier broke rank and ran up to the porch. As he handed the old woman a can of rations, she plunged a knife into his chest, killing him instantly.

A layer of sweat lacquered Chad's forehead as he continued walking down 56th. He would always remember the dead soldier's frozen expression of surprise. Chad had violated his own code now. But this is New York, a voice heckled from deep inside. It didn't matter, he argued.

As he crossed the street, he realized how short his breath had become. That had been one of Margaret's complaints over the past few weeks. Every time she climbed the stairs to their bed-

32

room, her chest heaved. Chad slowed down his own breathing consciously. The act of altering his respiration helped him reassert his control. He wondered whether his wife could do the same. Back again on the sidewalk, he straightened his already centered, well-knotted tie and buttoned the middle button of his finely tailored suit, then opened the heavy oak door to the Pied Piper Restaurant.

It was dark inside, forcing him to raise his arm toward an antique lantern and squint to see his watch. Twelve twenty-five. Five minutes early. Hoping he had arrived before Erik, Chad stole a quick glance into the smoke-filled interior. No signs of his friend amid the business men and women locked into the intensity of possible sales and contract details, their scenarios bouncing across each table with varying repercussions. When Chad scanned the room a second time, two customers caught his eye. As they waved their hellos, he forced a broad smile.

"Emery! Sid!" he called, not wanting to become any more intimate with his greeting.

"Thataway, Chad," Emery mouthed as he flashed a victory sign. Chad nodded his head, acknowledging the compliment. An article in *Scientific American* had featured his company's latest products as innovative and highly reliable. Emery and Sid worked for a competing corporation, one whose size and resources should have long ago crushed Millen's tiny factory as a viable competitor.

Usually, Chad looked forward to his business lunches at the Pied Piper. Henry, the maître d', was fond of him and, invariably, reserved a corner table for him. He enjoyed bringing clients there because Henry exhibited a great deal of *savoir-faire*, which made Chad feel like a visiting dignitary. But, today, neither Henry nor the friendly hand-waves mattered much to Chad. He kept thinking about Margaret. If he left work a little earlier, he calculated, it would still be six more hours until he would arrive home. Perhaps if he immersed himself into revising some of the production schedules, the time would pass more quickly. In any case, he would get through it; he always did.

33

"Has Mr. Spenser arrived yet, Henry?" he queried the tall, dapper man standing at the counter by the phone.

"Yes, Mr. Millen. He's at the bar." Henry smiled graciously. "Mr. Millen, would you care to be seated at your table and I will have Mr. Spenser join you there?"

Chad patted Henry on the shoulder. "That would be fine. Thank you."

When Erik sat beside his friend, his boisterousness punctured Chad's pensive mood.

"Hey, Chad, my man, good to see you."

They exchanged hearty handshakes.

"You know, I think you lost some weight," bellowed Erik. "Now, c'mon Chad, you wouldn't be dieting, would you?"

Chad laughed. "Nope. Don't believe in it. You know I'm only four pounds heavier than when I married Maggie." He nodded his head proudly, thankful to be enveloped by the conversation.

At about the time the waiter delivered the coffee and Erik expounded on his next business venture, Chad's interest waned.

"Maybe I'm getting too old," Erik stated. "Who knows? But I figure getting a little company like that on its feet and in the black has got to be a cinch after running 'the monster' for twelve years."

"Sure," Chad agreed, half-listening.

"Two years, I figure. All I need is two years . . . and then I'll be in the big money." Erik sighed at the thought, then continued. "This is probably the most brilliant idea I've ever had. Don't you think?"

This time all Chad could muster was "Mmmm-hmm."

Erik frowned. "Chad, where are you?"

Chad tried to focus on the question. "Sorry, Erik, I've just got a lot of things whirling around in my brain. You know, it's one of *those* kind of days." Verbal idioms and generalizations had been the mainstay of their relationship for fifteen years.

"Wait a minute," chimed Erik, jabbing himself in the head. "I don't believe what a jerk I am." His voice dropped an octave and softened noticeably. "Tell me, how's Maggie."

"Oh fine. Real fine."

"Good," Erik affirmed. "Glad to hear it." He paused and softened his voice once again. "Anything you want to talk about . . . you know I'm here."

"Thanks, Erik," Chad replied, "but, really, there's nothing to talk about. I mean, you know Maggie. This thing's not going to lick my girl. Right?"

Overzealously, Erik spurted, "Right! Absolutely!" He searched for more supporting thoughts. "You're something else, Chad. You've always been strong. That's one thing about you . . . STRONG!"

Chad could relate to that. Strong! He smiled to himself, then said, "Hey, listen, I made it through half of Vietnam on my belly . . . didn't I? I'll get through this one."

They both sat in silence, nodding their heads up and down. Erik stared at an indeterminate point at the far end of the room. Chad's fingers tapped out a marching rhythm on the table.

6 ⚘

Molded wood cabinets with brass handles lined two walls of the modernized kitchen. The stucco ceiling, painted pastel yellow, complemented the bright lemon-colored wallpaper. Margaret sat at the long wooden table pasting photographs into an album. The prints depicted handicapped schoolchildren. She smiled and pondered each photograph, then glued it into the book. A noisy lot, she mumbled affectionately. Whenever she'd enter the classroom, they'd shout to her with their small voices.

"Hey, Maggie, look at what I can do."

"I moved my leg, Maggie."

"Been exercising, Maggie, just like you said."

The buzzer on the digital clock startled her. Margaret slipped out of her chair and lunged for the counter. Alarms jarred her, especially those set by Chad. He had purchased this little electronic wonder because of its capability to trigger multiple alarm settings in one day. He would set it each morning to sound at regular intervals as a reminder for his wife to take her medication.

"Okay, okay," she clamored as she struggled to turn the tiny knob and silence the piercing whine. Quiet returned to the room. Margaret filled a glass with water, then popped open the tops of five pill vials, extracting one pill from each. Then, performing a familiar ritual, Margaret whipped the capsules into her mouth, following each with a slug of water, an exaggerated swallow, and a cringe. As she returned the glass to the sink, she glanced casually at the pamphlet accompanying one of her latest prescriptions. She read a couple of notations listed in the portion of the literature titled "Side Effects." Maggie shook her head in disbelief.

Suddenly, a convulsive charge of nausea ripped through her digestive tract. Margaret found herself holding tightly onto the kitchen counter as her body heaved and swayed. The lightheadedness increased. She didn't want to faint, but couldn't deny the sensation consuming her. Grabbing for the back of the chair, she allowed her legs to fold slowly under her so as to lower her body gently into her seat. I'll be okay now, she told herself, patting the wood frame and scolding herself for having rushed the clock. Margaret held her position for several minutes and stared out the window.

The sunshine filtering through the glass panes made the predominantly yellow kitchen even yellower. Mom would have loved it, she thought. Every morning, she and her mother would spend the opening hour of each day talking and laughing at the kitchen table. Then, at seven-thirty sharp, Katie, who had been crippled as a young child in an automobile accident, grabbed her metal-tipped cane from the closet and trudged out the door to work, leaving her daughter alone to finish breakfast. Raucous music from a neighboring apartment and the honks and screams from the street below became her morning symphony.

Maggie had lived on the fifth floor of a six-story walk-up tenement building in Brooklyn. The one thing she loved about her home was the kitchen window which overlooked the beach; if she squinted, she could catch the white caps of the waves pounding against the narrow strip of sand on the other side of the boardwalk. The ocean never changed, she would tell herself consolingly. In the summer, late at night when the shroud of darkness muted the sounds in the city streets, she would hang out the window to listen to the muffled thunder of the surf.

Although she loved being in the kitchen as a child, Margaret would, nevertheless, avoid looking at the dirty sink, its once-white enamel exposing large areas of black metal beneath it. She would try to ignore the rattles of the decrepit refrigerator, pitted from years of neglect and almost always empty. What she always remembered was the hugs she shared with her mother in that special room.

When Jake Shriner renovated the Four-Clover Bar across the street, he gave Maggie and her mother an old upright piano. The large, imposing instrument became Margaret's best friend. Fat Anthony Fontana, with his garlic breath and rumpled shirt, gave her lessons faithfully each week in trade for dinner on Mondays and Fridays. After school, Margaret would spend endless hours at the keyboard. Her mother would often sit beside her and listen admiringly as she practiced her scales. "Maggie," she'd say, "God talks through your hands." Then Katie took her daughter's palms and rubbed them lovingly against her own face.

Margaret's talent soon outstripped her first music teacher's knowledge. Katie, recognizing the problem, found a suitable replacement. Young Arthur Moorecraft, then a music professor at Brooklyn College, took Maggie on as his private student. Her long, sleek fingers became a perfect match for the complex fugues and sonatas she mastered. Margaret played for her mother, herself, and for the ocean. Oftentimes, she'd imagine the two of them on a sandy beach, dancing along the water's edge. Her mother's legs would be straight and firm. Together, they would move like swans. The sun would caress their graceful forms, growing warmer and warmer, yellower and yellower. The quickening rhythm of the dance would propel both of them into a spin; the circles growing ever smaller until they dropped to the sand and lay, face up, smiling at the sun.

That daydream capped every morning meal for young Margaret. Only after replaying each detail would she be satisfied to turn her vision toward the stream of light making its way lazily through parts of the dark, worn kitchen. It was at that time of her life, she presumed, that the color yellow had first taken on its significance. Yellow—the sun, life, warmth, the magical dance on the beach. One day she promised herself that she would have a vibrant yellow kitchen with, perhaps, a wall of windows enticing the sun to create a room of gold.

Margaret's father died just after her third birthday. The only memory of him she still carried with her was the day he brought her a chocolate heart wrapped in red paper. Maggie never ate it. It was far too beautiful and special. Instead, she kept it sitting on the bedroom bureau until the chocolate crumbled and became infested with bugs. She cried for hours when her mother finally threw it away. A week later, her father died of a heart attack.

When Chad gave her a candy heart on their fifth date, tears cascaded down her cheeks. Chad never knew why. According to all the stories her mother told her through the years about her father, this young man had many of the same qualities. Maggie liked that. Six months later, they married. When Katie passed away the following year, Maggie felt part of herself die with her. No more special smiles. No more talks by the window overlooking the sandy beach. No more mischievous giggles remembering fat Anthony Fontana. Death was so final. The only way to keep Katie alive would be to hold onto every last memory. Even now, she could see her mother leaning on her cane as she polished the face of the old upright piano.

A sharp pain in her abdomen brought Margaret's attention back to her own light-streaked, yellow kitchen. She inhaled and exhaled a short series of shallow breaths until it passed. Her body relaxed; the dizziness from before had substantially faded. She leaned over the photograph album and nodded. Maybe that's the reason I first went to St. Dominick's, she thought. Her mother had been like these children, crippled and, in some way, unwanted by her parents. Margaret could touch her mother and find that same, special intimacy every time she embraced one of her handicapped students. She would have given anything to hug just one of them right now.

As she picked up the photo of Eddie, the moisture filling her eyes blurred her vision. She brushed the tears away with the back of her hand in order to see his face more clearly. The laughing boy, his head tilted to one side, sat defiantly in a wheelchair. In his hand, which curled awkwardly in front of his chest, he held the ace of hearts. Margaret touched the shiny surface of the photograph and remembered Eddie before the laughter.

The wheelchair had been pushed up to a center table in the classroom. Eddie threw his arms wildly at the books and other games. Although he could barely control his hands, he managed to knock several lotto sets to the floor and disrupt the entire lesson. Margaret heard about the incident later. When she entered the classroom the following day, Eddie sat alone at a corner table, staring sadly at the wall.

"And you, Eddie," Maggie said, kneeling beside the youngster, "how's my champ doing?"

Eddie turned to her with his huge, lazy eyes. "Ain't talked to nobody yet . . ."

Margaret nodded. "Well, that's okay . . . but why not?"

"Nobody . . . cares about me."

"Nobody?" She lifted up his bent hand and caressed it to her cheek just as her mother had once done with her. "Well, I care about you, Eddie Xavier Chapman. I sure do."

He stared right into her eyes. "And that's why I talk to you, Maggie Millen."

The doorbell shocked Margaret out of her daydreaming. As she made her way slowly across the kitchen, she ran her fingers through her hair like a comb. She forced her body to straighten from the more comfortable bent position it had come to assume recently.

The entry foyer, dominated by a winding staircase to the second floor and a small settee in the corner, had been Margaret's pride when she and Chad refurbished the old colonial. The slate floor had been completely restored, the molding stripped to its original luster, and the walls papered in a discreet floral pattern. Margaret stopped before reaching the door, picked the newspaper off the stairs and her son's jacket off the banister, and deposited both in the closet. After one last, habitual glance around the room, she opened the door.

Margaret beamed. "I hoped you'd come today," she said to Janet, a pretty woman in her late thirties who had draped her trim, athletic form in a most stylish tennis outfit.

"In the flesh, sweetie," her friend answered, touching her cheek to Maggie's and kissing the air. "Let's have a look. Just what I thought. We have to get you out of this house before you turn green. Okay?" Before Margaret could answer, Janet continued. "How about I chauffeur you to the club and we watch the other girls play tennis?"

"Oh, Jan, I appreciate it, but . . . I honestly don't feel too well."

"Ah . . . that's okay," assured Janet. She charged into the foyer, deposited her pocketbook on the table, and twirled around to face her friend. "The tournaments are over anyway." A pause. "I didn't really want to go either."

"You go, Janet. I'll be fine here. You enjoy it so much. Go!"

Janet was tempted to say yes, okay, just this time, but before she could answer, her friend began to cough uncontrollably.

Margaret tried to suppress the spasm unsuccessfully, finally closing her eyes and trying to breathe deeply until it passed. When she looked up finally, she couldn't help but notice Janet's frightened expression.

"Sorry, Janet," she whispered as she touched her friend's arm reassuringly and squeezed out a faint smile. "It's okay. Don't worry, I'll be fine."

"Oh, I'm sure of that," Janet lied, searching for an acceptable exit line.

"How about a cup of coffee?" Margaret asked as she headed for the kitchen.

Janet chased after her. "I'll do it."

"Don't be silly," Margaret said smiling. "I'm not an invalid."

"Of course not!" Janet snapped.

Margaret set out two cups and poured the coffee. Janet, after eyeing herself in a small mirror and adjusting some strands of hair, perused the kitchen for something interesting to mention. Spotting the photographs on the table, she blurted, "Hey, aren't those the kids you worked with at the school?"

"Sure are," Margaret answered proudly. She arranged some pastries on a plate and set it on the table.

Janet picked up several of the prints and studied them. "Ah. The poor things."

"They're not 'poor things,' Jan. They just have difficulties doing certain activities."

"Oh, I know," Janet said half-listening as she glanced at the clock before returning her attention to the conversation. "Maggie, which one's Eddie?"

"This little guy," she chimed, putting her cup down and pointing at his photo. "He's something, isn't he? Oh, I miss them so—especially Eddie."

"Well, you'll be back to your old self in no time—running around, doing more than you have time for—I know you."

"Yeah, well, I hope so," Margaret responded. She peered out the window, then looked back to her friend. "You know, it's hard just staying home . . . relaxing." Maggie focused on Eddie's picture once more, then pushed it quickly into the book and closed it.

"Aw, sweetie," Janet said softly as she jumped up and hugged her friend. "Don't let it get to you now." An awkward pause. "And no more depressing talk." Janet returned to her seat and snapped her fingers. "I got it. How about a game of backgammon? Last time you whipped me, you fox, but today, I feel in rare form." She put out her hand. "Accept my challenge?"

Margaret nodded. "Thanks."

"Whatever for?"

Margaret shrugged her shoulders; her eyes filled with tears.

Janet stared at her friend and clasped her hands in front of her mouth. "You're going to make me cry and there's no sense to that, no sense at all." She touched Margaret's arm. "You sit.

I'll get the backgammon set. I know where it is." Janet darted from the kitchen.

The warm sunshine streaming through the windows caressed Margaret's hand, but she didn't notice as she sat, very alone, in her yellow kitchen and stroked the closed album on the table.

The sound of keys jiggled in the door. The latch snapped back as the lock released. Chad entered slowly, using his foot to push the door open. In one hand, he carried a small machine about the size of a miniature portable TV set. In his other hand, he held a leather attaché case that Margaret had bought him for his last birthday. Bending down on one knee, he set his satchel on the polished, oak floor while maintaining a firm grip on the oscilloscope. Chad dusted the debris left by his shoe on the door. Satisfied with the restoration, he closed the door, lifted his case, and stood up.

"Hello," he shouted, "I'm home. Maggie, I'm home."

"Hi," a voice called from the second floor. "Your mother left one of her gourmet meals in the kitchen."

Chad smiled. "That old pinch hitter always comes through."

Sam, a pencil over his ear and a book in hand, entered the foyer from the den.

"Hi, Pop."

Chad set the machine down carefully on the hall table before replying. "Well, here it is." He touched the instrument's circular scope with unmistakable reverence, then ran his index finger affectionately along one of the grid lines crisscrossing the screen. The sophisticated modular form seemed misplaced amid the lyrical watercolors on the walls and the Louis XV French provincial furniture in the room.

"It's the first one off the line," Chad said. "Just came up this afternoon. This is it! This is the baby I've been telling you about."

"Ah, great," Sam said. "Uh, Pop, could we talk?"

Chad whipped around playfully. His face sported a huge grin. No one could diminish his pleasure with this third generation scope that he, himself, had participated in designing. Loosening his tie, he crouched at the knees and assumed a prizefighting pose. Chad tucked his chin into his shoulder and pantomimed a few jabs toward his son.

"C'mon, c'mon," Chad shouted.

Sam fielded some punches lamely. Each time he backed away, his father pursued him. When Sam turned, Chad opened his right hand and tapped his son in the abdomen, then the side, then the top of his head.

"You're not much of an opponent today, huh?" Chad drove past Sam's right hand and flicked his fingers across his son's chin. "You gotta keep your right up more."

Sam pulled his right fist into a preset position in order to protect his face. The gesture seemed automatic, as if his limbs, by themselves, responded to his father's cues.

Chad smiled. "That'a boy."

Ducking to his left, Sam threw a hook past his father's arm and hit him lightly in the chest. The man laughed proudly. Suddenly, Sam looked at his clenched hands. They had become disconnected, unruly partners. He sighed and dropped his arms to his side.

"You got some time?" he asked his father.

"Sure, but let me say hello to your mother first." Chad pivoted like a spirited athlete and took the first four stairs in one grand leap. Using the railing for support, he proceeded to climb two steps at a time. "Start heating up the food," he bellowed, "and, oh, bring the SP₃ into the kitchen."

Sam shrugged his shoulders, a gesture which caught Chad's eye. He stopped momentarily at the top of the landing. "The SP₃ . . . that's the oscilloscope." A second later, he disappeared into the bedroom.

As Sam approached the machine, he heard his father's voice. "How's the prettiest girl in town doing today?" Chad asked in a strong, theatrical voice. He never heard his mother answer since she usually spoke in a much softer tone these days. Sam lifted the scope, surprised at its light weight.

The kitchen table had been set for three people. Each napkin had been carefully folded and flared like a seashell in front of each place setting. Salt and pepper shakers, ketchup, and numerous other accessories filled the center of the table. A huge glass bowl contained a voluptuous salad. Matching flasks housed a selection of salad dressings. Sam surveyed the table as he entered with the oscilloscope. "Grandma's banquet," he said to the walls.

Prior to his mother's illness, Sam never talked to himself, at least not out loud. He even scoffed at others who did. But, now, he began to find his own voice a welcome companion. Sometimes, the silence scared him.

Mimicking the care his father displayed in handling the instrument, he set the machine on the table, then flipped on the switches at the top of the stove, igniting the burners beneath the pots. He then withdrew two potholders from the drawer and placed them neatly on the counter. Usually, when it was his responsibility to prepare dinner, he never took the same interest. But, somehow, his grandmother's input always made the meal festive. "Ah ha," he said aloud, "not perfect." Without hesitation, he whipped a large knife from the rack and deposited it beside the uncut loaf of bread.

Sam seated himself in front of the oscilloscope. The crisp white lines drawn on the green screen looked like graph paper on glass. Twelve black dials had been arranged in two rows at the base of the small enclosure. Sam banged on it lightly with his knuckle. He couldn't decide whether it was plastic or metal. All the edges had been rounded like the heel of a good running sneaker, he thought. That metaphor enabled him to relate to the efficiency of such design. Yet, on some level, machines seemed alien to him—repetitious, predictable, unfeeling. Machines don't laugh, they don't cry. But some people don't laugh or cry either, Sam decided. He tried to imagine what it must be like working all day with transistors, wires, electrical currents, and little dancing dots.

"A beauty, isn't she?" Chad said as he entered the kitchen.

"Looks impressive," Sam had to admit. Alien, but impressive.

Chad turned a chair around and sat on it backward as he faced the table. "What you can't see is even more impressive than what you can see."

"Dad, uh, is Mom's anemia catching?"

Chad raised his eyebrows, startled by the question. "No, of course not. Where did you get such a crazy notion?"

Sam shrugged his shoulders.

Chad placed one arm around his son and pointed to the machine. "You got to stay focused, Sam. On the beam, as they say." He paused, withdrew his arm and stared at the oscilloscope. "That kind of discipline enabled us to make this little baby. Once we get into full production, it'll be the fastest, lightest portable in the business. This puts us on the same level as the big boys." He opened a panel on the side of the unit, revealing jack outlets. "No one has a plug-in section like this. You can tap into any computer, feed in or out. Distortion factor in any cycle is less than zero point four percent." Chad closed the panel. "Now that's mind-boggling."

Obviously, Sam did not understand everything his father said, but he was swept into the commentary because of Chad's intensity.

Putting his hand on Sam's shoulder, he continued. "And it's darn near indestructible, too." His voice dropped to a whisper. "This scope can withstand every shock conceivable. Drop it under the water, up to five thousand feet and it will still work. Put it in the oven, turn it up to five hundred degrees and nothing will happen." He smiled. "The strong survive. You remember that, Sam, you hear?"

Sam peered into his father's eyes, hesitated, then finally nodded his head.

Chad stroked the machine. "Solid. Reliable. Steady. Most important, it won't foul up under pressure."

"Sounds just like you, Chad," Margaret said as she stood in the doorway smiling.

Both Chad and Sam looked up startled.

Margaret had put the finishing touches on her makeup, combed her hair, and dabbed some perfume around her neck.

Despite her bathrobe, her grooming appeared impeccable. She bowed playfully to her husband and son.

Chad rose from the chair quickly, but not too quickly. He smiled as he approached his wife. She slipped her arm gently around his and he assisted her in walking to the table.

"What do you think?" he asked, his eyes riveted once again on the SP_3. "Isn't it everything I told you? Isn't it?"

"Quite an accomplishment," she answered as she slowly lowered herself into her seat. "When you set your mind to something, it amazes me."

Chad helped Sam bring the steaming pots to the table. "It wasn't only me, you know. A lot of guys worked on this one." As he began to serve his wife, he glanced at the machine. "Indestructible!"

"Indestructible, huh?" Margaret mused. "Not like people, I guess."

Chad almost responded, but stopped himself. He sat down in his chair and began to eat mechanically. He couldn't look up at his wife. Sam, in contrast, peered at his mother as she forced herself to eat. Margaret returned her son's watchfulness with a soft smile.

"Well now, Sam," she said, "tell me about everything that happened in school today."

Sam nodded. He did not disappoint his mother. He told her all the details; his tests, new lessons, teachers' expressions, the behavior of his friends. Unpleasant facts, such as his encounter in the lunchroom with Hank and Bud, were omitted. He couldn't remember how he knew to censor certain experiences. As he talked, Sam Millen thought fleetingly about his father's reliable little machines and wondered whether he, too, had become a plugged-in, button-operated device with certain preprogrammed and prescribed areas of operation.

7 ✄

A six-foot pencil and several four-foot clothespins hung from the ceiling on which a naturalistic skyscape had been painted, complete with a misty blue field, clouds, even the underbelly of a passing airplane. Radios in the form of Coke bottles, mugs shaped like human breasts, Zippo cigarette lighters nine inches tall, five-pound chocolate candy Kisses, and red-hot lips doubling as down-filled pillows cluttered the shelves in one small section of the store. Lisa kept twirling around, unable to let her vision rest on one item. She darted to the glass-enclosed cabinet and stared at miniaturized human parts which had been molded artfully into ceramic toothbrushes.

"They're so silly," Lisa laughed. "How'd you find this place?"

Jessica had not followed her to the other side of the room; nevertheless, she heard the question. "You're in good hands . . . as the saying goes," she quipped while continuing to peruse a colorfully illustrated book entitled *Uncommon Trivia*. Her short, black hair had been swept back rather severely off her face. No makeup adorned the strong, sculptured features which appeared almost frozen in a stone mask. As a youngster, Jessica hated being tall, but now she accented that very attribute, oftentimes elevating her form with four-inch heels.

Lisa picked up an oversized matchbox. She opened the container and shook her head. All the match sticks had been cut into risqué human forms bent in compromising positions. "I don't think so," she said softly as she moved closer to her friend. "Did you really think we could buy the gift here?"

Jessica rolled her eyes. "I sure did."

Lisa shook her head again. At that moment, a salesman intervened. "Can I help you ladies?"

"Yes," Jessica answered. "My friend is looking for something much more provocative."

"Jessie," Lisa snapped. "No, no," she countered to the young man smiling at her. "What I'd like is something a little less . . ."

". . . provocative?" he asked.

"Yes, I guess that's a good way to put it."

Jessica placed her body purposely between her friend and the salesman. After an awkward moment, he directed them to a more sedate section of the store.

"Boring," Jessica chimed each time he lifted a potential gift off the shelf. "B-o-r-i-n-g."

"No, no, show me," Lisa countered, becoming uncomfortable with Jessie's attitude. She worried about offending the salesclerk.

"How about this?" he continued unruffled.

Lisa studied the Lucite desk clock, then shook her head. "Not right, but thanks." She nodded, smiled and then asked, "Is there something that falls in between those weird toothbrushes and this clock?"

"Okay, ladies, follow me."

When Lisa trailed after him obediently, Jessica steamed. She had driven Lisa all around the city only to watch her be led like a leashed puppy by what she assessed as a simpleton salesclerk.

Finally, Lisa settled on a gift quite hesitantly. She wanted to please Jessica, to break her own molds, yet she felt confined by her dominance and pushing. Jessie and her dad had many things in common, she thought.

At the cash register, the young man who had assisted them asked Lisa, very discreetly, for her phone number. Jessica, her eyes narrowed and her jaw thrust forward, glared at her friend. Although Lisa declined graciously to give out any information, she appreciated the warmth and attention.

Once in the street, Jessica grabbed her arm. "Could I have your number, pretty lady? Oh please, please!"

"C'mon, Jessie, don't make a big deal out of it."

Jessica knew she had reacted unrealistically, had pulled the trigger too soon, but, somehow, she couldn't retrieve her comments or even soften them with a flimsy retraction. Instead, she pushed away from her friend and walked ahead.

Lisa ran after her, catching up to her at the corner. "Would *you* like my phone number?" she whispered playfully to Jessica as they both waited for the traffic light to change. No response. "Well, it's 755-3266."

"I think that's my phone number too," her friend replied, allowing a thin smile to soften her expression.

"How convenient," Lisa whispered as she tapped Jessica's arm. The "walk" sign flashed. Together, they proceeded across the street.

The mature plantings and towering old trees camouflaged the angularity of the square half-acre behind the Millen house. Ivy had consumed the exterior of the ancient cedar fence which had been constructed in a colonial style to match the handsome two-story structure it surrounded. Every ten feet, a square post topped with an ornate decorative platform reached beyond the leaves like stately sentries from a distant era. The gardens bridging the two patios beside the house had been purposely cropped in order not to interfere with any limited views afforded through the four sets of French doors leading to the backyard. Today, they all had been opened wide, allowing for an easy flow from the living room and dining room to the entertaining areas on either side of the outdoor, brick barbecue pit. Frank Sinatra's voice belted out from exterior speakers mounted discreetly beneath the lower ledges of the roof. Some friends and relatives had gathered in small groups inside and outside of the house. Laughter and the popping corks from bottles of sparkling wine accented the party atmosphere.

Chad, wearing a blue plaid apron, poked the sizzling steaks on the grill. He kept regulating the flame by fastidiously adjusting the cast-iron vents. Erik set out plates on the cement counter, then began withdrawing cooked potatoes from the fire. Sam delivered the first platters to some of the guests. Janet, her body straining against form-fitting pants, demonstrated by pantomine her best tennis serve to an admirer. Myrna refilled drinks, cheerfully entering and exiting conversations. Margaret, dressed in a new suit, lounged on a chaise. Charlie Millen sat beside her, holding his hands out, palms up, as if to hold the rays of the sun. The gentle heat tickled his flesh. He purred like an old house cat, stealing a glance at his daughter-in-law. She giggled. Charlie knew he could always make her laugh. Besides, Charlie believed in laughter as the route to health and, failing that, the only sensible route to heaven.

"Now this here weather didn't just happen, Maggie, no sir," he said with great conviction as he pointed up to the sky. "By God, it came as a special order. I've been working on it for six days." He held up ten fingers, then noticed his error. "Ten days that is."

Margaret squeezed his arm. "Six days, ten days. It doesn't matter. A girl couldn't ask for a better birthday present. Thanks, Pop." She kissed him, then relaxed against the upright portion of the chaise. Margaret extended her hands like Charlie had, then looked up. "There's a painting in the Metropolitan with a sky that looks just like this. Big white clouds on a blue, blue field. Every time I see that painting, I get this deep down feeling—real peaceful." She sighed, her face breaking into a full smile. "Just like now. It's my favorite kind of day." Margaret took her father-in-law's hand and kissed it. "Thanks, Pop."

"You haven't seen nothin'," he insisted.

Renee, a neighbor, and Sally, one of the women Margaret used to play tennis with, strolled over to the chaise.

"Your husband's quite a cook, Maggie," Sally volunteered. "Any time you ever want to rent him out, just let us know."

"He comes very expensive," Margaret replied. Charlie touched her shoulder and slipped away.

"It's very brave of you to celebrate birthdays," said Renee. "Unless, of course, we start counting backward." Both she and Renee laughed.

Margaret smiled thoughtfully. "You know, I'd never thought I'd say this, but I like getting older. Wouldn't trade my twenties for my thirties." She glanced down at her hands. "Old hands though . . . I've always had old hands."

"What you need is more wine," Renee said abruptly. "More wine over here," she shouted to Myrna, who refilled the glasses. "Now, I'll tell you about the scores the girls had in the weekend tournament. Francine and Rhoda won three out of . . ."

"Happy birthday, Mom," Lisa said enthusiastically as she and Jessica entered the yard through the kitchen. After planting a kiss on her mother's cheek, Lisa smiled her hello to Renee and Sally, then introduced her friend to them.

"Happy birthday, Maggie," Jessica said softly.

"Thank you . . . both of you."

"Here, for her highness," Lisa countered, placing a narrow rectangular box into her mother's lap.

Margaret smiled at the caricature drawn on the wrapping paper. Lisa had sketched the members of her family holding an infant Margaret on their shoulders and cheering. The comic book blurb said, "You're not getting older, you're getting smarter."

"That's good, really good," Renee said, admiring the drawing.

"Can I open it?" Margaret asked.

"Of course," Lisa laughed.

"I want to save the drawing," Margaret said as she lifted the tape from the corners of the package. Everyone waited quietly as she unwrapped the gift. A box, containing a paper towel roll, was unveiled. The bold type announced the contents: "Dieter's

Guide to Weight Loss During Sex." Margaret glanced up at Lisa surprised, then shrugged her shoulders like a little girl and laughed. Both Renee and Sally appeared more tentative about their responses.

Lisa hugged her mother. "I know it's a bit risqué, but I wanted something cheerful."

"Mission accomplished," Margaret said emphatically. "But I'm not sure cheerful is exactly the right word." She winked at her daughter. "Well, we might as well see what we have here."

The women gathered around her as she withdrew the roll and began to read the inscriptions. Sally, despite herself, was the first to laugh. "Shouldn't we read it aloud," she said.

Margaret looked over at Chad, then shook her head. "Ladies, I think we'd do better making this a silent reading lesson."

After everyone had finished eating, the group reassembled in the living room. In spite of the ornate fireplace, the focal point of the room appeared to be the small baby grand piano. Both the antique love seats and the tufted couch faced it. An assortment of chairs had also been turned in the same direction.

A mammoth oriental rug accented the floral motif of the upholstered furniture as well as the curtains. Flowers from the garden had been placed in the vases on the mantel above the fireplace. A dozen long-stemmed roses, from Chad, decorated the top of the piano. Margaret admired them as she sat on the bench facing the keyboard.

"Do *Peer Gynt*, honey," Chad requested.

"How about a jig?" blurted Charlie, who lifted his hands, ready at a moment's notice to begin dancing.

Laughter filled the room.

"Hush up," Myrna whispered to her husband.

Margaret turned to her guests. "First *Peer Gynt*, then a jig, then we'll take requests."

Several people applauded; a few shouted, "Here! Here!" Charlie elbowed his wife and giggled.

As those in the room became silent, Margaret ran the tips of her fingers across the keys. Her expression became very serious. And then she began. Her fingers danced easily across the keyboard. A soft smile enveloped her face.

Chad eased back into his chair. He found the music reassuring. It followed a logical set of principles, much like those which order electronics and engineering. Chad enjoyed anticipating each melodic sequence, even before his wife struck the notes.

Lisa moved her head with the cadence of the music. She knew her mother could have been a concert pianist; that she had side-stepped a special talent for the American dream—husband, house, and family. She knew she would never have the same conflict.

From a distant corner, Sam watched attentively, his fingers nervously twirling a loose button on his shirt. Every time his mother played the piano, he would watch her face and notice unfamiliar expressions emerge. The contour of her lips jutted out a touch more than usual from her face. Her eyes had a fiery glow. Strands of hair broke away from their ordered position and danced haphazardly in front of her face. Sam imagined if he called to her at that moment she would answer in a deep, resonant voice, a strange voice, not his mother's voice. A moment of panic tightened every muscle in his body. Something kept changing right before his eyes, something he couldn't define or explain. Sam Millen began to suspect that he didn't really know the woman who had mothered him . . . yet he wanted to, almost desperately, now more than ever before.

Myrna oozed with pride as she watched her daughter-in-law perform; but Charlie, sitting beside her, appeared preoccupied; perhaps he awaited his jig. Janet and her husband Erik sipped vodka tonics as they listened. This marked the first time they were together all afternoon. Several people leaned against the back of the sofa. Not only were all the seats in the living room occupied, but some guests found suitable places for themselves on the floor.

Margaret's body rocked back and forth as her hands and arms and torso became an extended expression of the music.

The piano was an old friend. And the haunting melody of *Peer Gynt* provided her with a safe womb in which she could always retreat. She never needed the glory of applause or recognition, a fact which may have diminished her ambition far more than her marriage. The music had opened doorways to her feelings which had never quite found their expression in words.

Suddenly, Margaret missed a six-note progression with her right hand. Her fingers seemed to have collapsed as they met the face of the keys. She stopped playing immediately and stared at her hand. When she remembered the presence of an audience, she turned around self-consciously for an instant and smiled at blank faces. No one understood her reason for pausing. Margaret faced the piano again and shrugged her shoulders. She placed her fingers carefully over the keyboard and began the sequence again. As she extended her right hand in order to redo the same small section, it missed its mark. Her eyelids quivered as she lifted her hand and studied it as if it had been disconnected from her body.

This time, Chad realized what had happened. Work through it, he counseled her silently. C'mon, Maggie, work through it. Myrna considered helping Margaret, but lacking any concrete plan, decided instead to remain seated. Charlie still appeared adrift in his own thoughts; but not Sam and Lisa, who gaped at their mother. Neither of them had ever witnessed her having any difficulty with her music. In fact, that had always been the area, along with her teaching at St. Dominick's, in which she exhibited uncanny control and expertise.

Leaning forward once again, Margaret Millen began to play very slowly. The cadence was all wrong, but she seemed oblivious to that as well as the guests. With single-minded determination, she glared at her hands, compelling them to respond, but her fingers became rubbery a third time. Unmatched notes, sounding simultaneously, sent their shrill cries of dissonance through those gathered in the room. Chad stood up uncomfortably; his face fell into an automatic smile. At the same time, Charlie bounced to his feet, a fork and knife visible in his hands. As he scrambled around the coffee table and trotted across the room, he announced, "Have it fixed in no time flat." Several people laughed nervously.

The old man leaned over the opened side of the baby grand. He scratched his Basset hound jowls and squinted through his bushy eyebrows. His childlike gaze became studious as he began poking at the strings with his kitchen utensils. Myrna shook her head angrily, too embarrassed to retrieve her husband. She side-glanced at the other guests, then began to rub her chest. Without anyone noticing, Myrna deposited a nitroglycerin pill under her tongue.

Once again, Margaret positioned her hands and began to play. Once again, her aim was obviously off.

Janet leaned over to Erik. "I can't watch," she whispered, "please, let's leave." He resisted her request until she tugged on his sleeve, forcing him to stand.

Charlie, a touch more desperate now, pulled on the strings. Margaret ignored him. She flexed her fingers and began a fifth time, still without any success. Chad approached slowly. Several people exited through the glass door. Renee and Sally retreated into the kitchen. No one spoke. The notes on the piano kept sounding off in an unordered fashion as Margaret kept trying. Tears filled her eyes.

Touching her gently from behind, Chad said, "C'mon, sweetheart. All you need is a little rest."

The old man put his hand up. "Wait! A little more, Maggie, and I'll have it fixed. Stay with it," he begged, "and you'll see."

"Jesus, Pop," Chad barked.

Margaret smiled at the old man, who nodded and smiled back to her. After Chad led his wife from the room, Sam kept looking around, not knowing what to do or how to react. His face twitched with tension. Finally, he followed his parents.

As Chad ushered his wife into the bedroom with his son trailing behind, he stole several glances at her hands. It didn't make any sense, he told himself. Where's the damn logic? The medicine. It had to be the medicine again.

"Here, sit down," he counseled his wife. "Listen, even Rubinstein had his hits and misses."

Margaret touched her husband's hand and grinned wearily. "I'm okay." She nodded reassuringly to Sam. "Both of you, go back downstairs. Give me a couple of minutes in the bathroom; I want to freshen up. Okay?"

"You got it," Chad said smartly as he turned around. He tapped his son on the head and pointed to the door like a general. "Let's give the lady her privacy." They met Lisa in the hall. Chad never replied directly to his daughter's request for an explanation. He confidently dismissed her question and said, "Everything's under control now."

For Margaret, the solitude of the bedroom came as a welcomed relief. The muffled voices from the first floor no longer intruded. No more performances. No games. And yet she couldn't bear to rethink the incident in the living room. She had to go forward. In the bathroom, Margaret stood in front of the sink and faced herself in the mirror. She flexed her right hand, but couldn't bear to observe the movement directly. Instead, she fixed on the reflection. Her fingers moved in a predictable manner, although they did not have the resiliency or power they normally exhibited. Margaret made a fist and banged on the porcelain fixture. She winced at the pain in her hand, then faced the mirror arrogantly. Her eyes were bloodshot; her skin drawn and sallow. The defiance dwindled into disappointment. She touched her forehead and the skin around her eyes. Her fingers trembled when they pushed against the wrinkles growing more visible around her mouth. She had meant what she had said earlier to Renee and Sally. She would not have traded her thirties for her twenties. But, now, something else in her face disturbed her. The aging process seemed out of control, racing toward some unspeakable end. When she was seventeen, she admitted to having old, wrinkled hands, the genetic legacy of her family. What she saw now was different. Her fingers probed the skin underneath her chin and along her neck. Deep crevices had appeared in areas that had been smooth not long ago. A month? Two months ago? She couldn't be sure. Why hadn't she noticed them before, she asked herself. The light-headed sensation she experienced in the mornings returned, forcing her to lean against the sink for support.

"Hello, I'm Margaret Millen," she whispered into the mirror. "I'm not crazy or anything. It's just that I think I should talk to someone."

She shook her head, eradicating the pose. Inhaling deeply, she began again. "Hello, I'm . . . everything's okay, really. I'm sick, you see, but my husband and I are real positive thinkers."

Margaret swallowed noisily, pressed her hands against her mouth and stood frozen for several seconds. Then, slowly, ever so slowly, she let her arms drop to her sides. "Hello, my name's Maggie. You see, my family just had this birthday party for me and you see, I, I, always play . . . this piece . . . on the . . . piano . . ."

Margaret Millen bowed her head and cried.

The white bricks glistened in the late afternoon sun. A strong wind from the northwest made the tulips bordering the driveway cower. Chad fixed his collar as he waved to the last departing guests. "Take care." "The steaks were great!" "Thanks for having us." Only a few people dared to address the issue which cut the heart out of the party a full two hours before it ended officially. Sally said it first. "Hope Maggie feels better."

"Me too," Bob Carpenter, a neighbor, said as he exited the front door with his wife.

Myrna shouted orders frantically as Charlie hustled her down the driveway. "Chad, give her lemon and water tonight. Do as I say. The banana cake has to be wrapped and put away. And for God's sake, don't stand there like that, button your jacket."

"Shush up, you old fool," Charlie muttered as he opened the door to his car.

A few more stragglers pumped their host's hand, then scudded down the driveway to their cars. Finally alone, Chad ambled across the lawn and retrieved a few branches dislodged from the old trees by the strong gusts. He dumped them in a tall garbage can he acquired for that very purpose. He needed time before entering the house again, but he didn't know why. Chad bent down and cleared the grass away from a nozzle connected to the underground sprinkler system. He checked the shutters beside the large bay window, then scanned the roof. The aluminum valley the roofers had replaced two years ago still looked brand new. Maybe we'll tackle the drains in the fall, he counseled himself. He loved old colonials—solid, simple designs that lasted hundreds of years if constructed correctly. He had been the house's seventh owner. Chad Millen looked up at the trio of old oak trees at the side of his property and wondered who else would one day stand in his place, on this front lawn, admiring the same shrubbery and landscape. He pulled his shoulders back, turned and headed for the house.

Lisa and Jessica came out of the front door together.

"Good-bye, Mr. Millen," Jessica said. "Tell Maggie I hope she feels better tomorrow."

"I certainly will," Chad smiled.

Jessica walked ahead, leaving Lisa with her father.

"Dad . . . can't the doctor do anything?"

"They are," he said. "It's a slow process. We all have to be patient. She'll be fit as a fiddle again—you'll see."

Lisa walked her father up the driveway. She considered taking his arm, but hesitated.

"Maybe you should try some other . . . methods or something," she suggested.

Chad stopped abruptly. "Don't you think I've looked into everything? How dare you question me!"

"I'm not . . ."

"And also, young lady," he interrupted, visibly trying to control his fury, "that gift you gave your mother was in bad taste."

Lisa's lips quivered as she pressed her fingers against her temple. She wanted to hit him, she had always wanted to hit him, but, instead, she backed away from him without responding, finally turning and running down the driveway.

Chad turned angrily. As he faced his house, he noticed his son peering down at him from the bedroom window above the garage. They stared at each other for a few seconds, then Sam backed out of view.

When his American History section ended the following day, Sam, thankful for the final dismissal bell, separated from his classmates and walked across the fields bordering the southern boundary of the school grounds. He stopped at Leakman's pond and eyed the reflection of the clouds imprinted on the mirrorlike surface. Two students broke the reverie when they ran across a distant crest, laughing and shouting messages to each other. Why did all the kids always need company wherever they went? he wondered.

"Hey, Sam," they'd say, "I'm going to pick up something at the store for my mom. Wanna come along?"

Or if they wanted to practice their tennis backhand against the handball court wall, they would inevitably solicit companionship.

Sam treasured his quiet moments alone, especially on a day like today when a gentle breeze swayed the trees and teased his hair. Maybe he'd be able to sort some things out for himself. Maybe it would take away some of the pressures he felt. Maybe he could forget . . . for just awhile. Glad for the privacy, he assumed just about everyone had already caught the after-school bus home. It was getting more and more difficult to find a peaceful spot these days, he thought. Sam bent down, placed his books on the grass, then picked up the flattest rock he could find. Jerking his hand sideways and dipping into the movement, he spun the rock off, skimming the top of the water and counting the jumps it made. One. Two. Three. Four. Pretty good, he mused, but I can top it. He searched for another rock. Just as he discovered one with a wide, well-balanced, flat base, a distant figure on a bicycle drew his attention by calling his name. Sam squinted to see who it was. The figure grew larger and larger rapidly as it sped closer to him, doing wheelies as it ascended the slope toward the pond.

"Vell, hello dare," joked Brian in one of his ten favorite accents.

"Hey, Bri. What are you doing here? I thought everyone had deserted the ship by now."

"Came to see how the elephants are doing," Brian quipped.

Sam tried to be there with him, adding, "I think they went thatta'way," pointing across the pond.

Brian made wide circles around Sam with his bike, utilizing a different accent each time he spoke.

"Hey, you all heard wha ol' Tarzan said when he saw them elephants comin' over da hill?" he asked in an uneven southern drawl.

Sam shook his head "no" as he threw another rock into the pond. His muscles began to tense.

"Here come de elephants," Brian whooped, making another wheelie with his bike.

Sam forced a smile despite an intense urge to scream.

Using his normal voice, Brian kept at him. "Well, I'll try again. This one's bound to get you." He then ventured a Scottish brogue. "What did Tarzan say when he spied the elephants coming over the hill with sunglasses on? Nothin', m'lad. He didn't recognize 'em!"

No laugh came from Sam as he dropped to the grass awkwardly and held his hands, palms down, on the ground as if to balance himself. Brian stopped his bicycle and watched with a puzzled look on his face. Suddenly, he saw Sam's legs begin to shake. As they both became engrossed in the quivering, it spread to Sam's hands.

"What's the matter, Sam?" Brian asked.

Sam didn't answer. He jumped to his feet abruptly as if he had been stung, then gaped at his hands which were still vibrating.

"Gotta go," Sam spurted, trying desperately to sound casual. He bent down to retrieve his books and almost lost his balance. Scooping them clumsily into his arms, he jogged away without another word, leaving Brian a little scared and confused.

"Sam . . . Sam . . . !" he called after his friend, who never once turned around as he ran across a distant slope and disappeared behind the trees.

8 ⋄

Sam Millen came to see me three weeks after his mother's birthday party, though my involvement with his family began, tangentially, long before Margaret's illness. His grandfather, who had attended several of my lectures, recruited me to conduct workshops for the downtown Senior Citizens' Center (SCC). Charlie not only wedged his presence into every session, but also became adept at mimicking the kinds of questions I used in facilitating dialogues with others. What had been a lifestyle for me, as well as a therapeutic and educational process, became a crusade for Charlie Millen. He wanted to rid his peers of unhappiness in one quick thrust of his verbal saber. He lobbied for more smiles, more joy, and less concern about the future. But not everyone wanted his Nirvana, so the old man shrugged and threw down his sword.

"You can love them with your questions, Bears," he would say, "but I'd prefer to ignore them." Although he punctuated such remarks with mischievous laughter, he kept attending my sessions at SCC, ordaining himself, finally, as my assistant and liaison to the center.

Once, when I could not come to a meeting, he sat in my chair, wearing a rented beard and a rather long-haired wig. A box had been placed beside him so that he could approximate my six-foot-three-inch frame if he had to stand. Calling himself

63

my official clone for the evening, he imitated my rather demonstrative hand gestures as he asked the questions. Although most viewed his short reign as loving and reasonably nonjudgmental, several members, who fell victim to his impatience, harbored a distinctly different perspective. The woman whom he kept referring to as "Grand Goose Loony" hit him with her pocketbook at the end of the session.

"What do you do about the real crazies," he asked me the following week.

"Maybe you don't see them or their behavior as crazy. In their way, they're doing the best they can to take care of themselves . . . just like you and me. Would you want to condemn them for it?"

Charlie never answered; instead, he spent an entire day with "Grand Goose Loony," helping her in her garden while addressing her respectfully by her given name. A week later, he played imaginary music with an elderly gentleman who brought his invisible guitar to the center one day. No one applauded his gestures, but I sensed that this man did not require that kind of support.

Four months after the series ended, Charlie asked me to join him at a county park. As he launched six piggyback kites with remarkable skill, he told me about Sam. I agreed to see his grandson only if the youngster made the appointment himself and expressed his own desire. Charlie understood. Another two months passed before Sam made the phone call.

The initial segment of my first session with Sam Millen began in a small one-room structure wedged between maple and oak trees on a small hill behind my home. The Option House, as my children called it, had a wall of glass which caught the early morning sun. Inside, two rustic love seats faced one another across a butcher-block coffee table. A huge photograph of a dancer wearing worn ballet shoes and tattered leg warmers dominated one wall. A print of a kneeling, battle-fatigued soldier comforting an abandoned infant hung on another wall amid a grouping of abstract paintings. Additional panels of glass revealed the trees and foilage outside.

Sam draped his long legs across the coffee table, letting his hands dangle from the sides of the chair. The growth of his nose had outpaced the rest of his face, giving him an awkward, gangly appearance, though not diminishing the strength of his deep-set eyes and angular jaw. His curly hair had been cropped close to his head with little regard for style.

Silence reigned for the last fifteen minutes. Sam's face tensed. He tapped out a drum rhythm on the table, while glancing around the room nervously, hopping from object to object without any sustained interest. Finally, he said, "There's nothing wrong with stopping track. It's a dumb sport anyway."

"How do you feel about that?" I asked.

"Great! Fine, just fine," he insisted.

"Then why the question?"

"You know why. Okay, it's not a dumb sport. I like track. I'm the best long distance runner in the county. But . . . but I can't, not now. Not while Ma's sick."

"Why not?"

"I have to get home and help after school. We take turns. My sister even comes from Manhattan a couple of times each week. Do we have to talk about this?"

"Why? Does it upset you?"

"Yes. How can I feel better if all I think about is her being sick?" He turned his head. The muscles in his jaw tensed.

"What about it disturbs you?"

"The damn game. It's called the smile game. Before my mother got sick, we smiled at lots of things. Now we're supposed to smile at everything. But you know what . . . nobody really feels the smiles. They're silly and I can't stand them!"

"What is it about them that you can't stand?"

"It's a lie, everybody's lying—me, Dad, Sis. Everybody's so full of shit with my mother. Dad says it's just a matter of time until Ma gets better." Sam rubbed his hands together. "Two nights ago, when I showed her my biology project, she smiled . . . and I could see the blood between her teeth." He winced uncomfortably. "That's why I can't go back to track."

"Because of the blood between her teeth?" I asked.

"Well . . . like all those kinds of things."

"I'm not sure what you mean . . . how does that relate to track?"

"Hey, my mother's very, very sick," Sam said. "I care about her, know what I mean? How can I go out and spend time at track?"

"What is it about spending time at track that you see as not okay to do since your mother's sick?"

"It's like laughing and horsing around while someone in the next room is not well . . . it's like making fun."

"Do you believe that?"

"Yes," Sam said firmly.

"Why do you believe that?"

" 'Cause it's true."

"Okay . . . could you explain how it happens, how track would be making fun?"

He rose from the chair and walked out onto the deck. Sam shook his head like a young colt. Within seconds, he spun around and marched back into the room. "Look, track for me is having fun, having a good time. How could I have fun while she's so darn sick?"

"What do you believe that would mean?" I asked.

"That I didn't care."

"Why do you believe it would mean you didn't care?"

"When someone you care about doesn't feel good," he asserted, "You don't feel good either."

"Sammy, that might be your experience, but why does it happen?"

"It's natural."

"What do you mean?"

"That's the way it happens." He flopped down on the couch, his long limbs dangling in every direction.

"I understand that's what you have usually experienced," I said. "But what is it about your mother's feeling bad that makes you feel bad?"

"Because I don't want her to feel bad and be sick."

"Not wanting her to feel bad is very different than your feeling bad when she does. Why do you feel bad, Sammy?"

"I don't know any more. I'm getting confused. You ask the weirdest questions."

I smiled at him, then suggested, "Let me try another one on you. Sammy, what are you afraid would happen if you didn't feel bad when your mother did?"

"It'd mean I didn't care about her," he said, shaking his head as if denying his words.

"Do you believe that?"

"Yes. No. Maybe more no. Last week, we went to the countywide debating match. Our school placed second. I really had a great time, a fantastic time 'cause I knew my stuff cold. I was so into it, I forgot about everything. I wasn't feeling bad then, but I know I still, somehow, cared about Ma."

"So does having fun mean you don't care," I queried.

"I guess not. They're two different things. I can see that now. Guess I thought I was supposed to be miserable all the time."

"And now?"

"I don't have to do that."

Sam and I smiled at each other.

"C'mon," I said, "let's go for a walk."

As we entered the park, the ducks and geese quacked a welcoming chorus as they paddled across the lake toward us. Once they realized we were not game wardens coming to feed them, they turned away and chattered among themselves as if to make sense out of our intrusion. I mimicked some of their sounds in an effort to display our camaraderie. Sam watched me curiously, neither participating nor making a comment. We found a bench in the sun.

"You know, until you did that with the ducks, I couldn't quite see you and Grandpa together. Even so, you guys are about as opposite as two people can be."

"Really?" I laughed. "I think we're very much alike. Doing sessions with him at the SCC was quite an experience." A seagull hovered over us for a second, then soared, in a low glide, over the lake. "Your grandfather is what you might call—a free man. Not many people feel free these days." I tapped my head. "Freedom—that's a state of mind." I paused, then nodded my head. "Well, let's get back to you."

"To tell you the truth, I'm not used to talking like this," Sam said. He picked at a peeling chip of paint on the bench, sighed, then continued. "I keep thinking about what I said before. I might know it's okay not to be miserable, but everyone else won't understand; they'd be like I was before we talked. If they saw me laughing or horsing around, they'd think I didn't care."

"Who's they?"

"My dad, Sis, my friends at school. That'd be really awful!"

"Why?" I asked.

"Because it wouldn't be true."

"And if what they thought was untrue, why would that disturb you?"

"It wouldn't matter that it was untrue. I just wouldn't want them to think that."

"Why not?"

"I know it's going to sound stupid," he said, "but I'd feel embarrassed."

"Why, Sammy?"

"They'd, maybe, think bad things about me, not want to be with me, ignore me like a freak."

"Do you believe that?"

He looked away sheepishly, then adjusted his position on the bench. "No," he grinned, "not really. Boy, I say a lot of things I don't believe."

"Sometimes, Sammy, when we say and hear what we think, we can see it more clearly. Maybe that's why so many people talk to themselves, to get it out there and look at it."

"I'm the kind that doesn't talk to himself, at least not about serious things," he observed. "You know what I said before about them thinking I didn't care . . . well, I don't know if that's true. Maybe some would, you know, put me down . . .

68

that's a great sport in my class. At least Brian would understand. But what about Dad?''

''What about him?''

''He loves Ma so much, he's so miserable about what's going on . . . I mean, underneath all those smiles. He wouldn't understand about track. He'd tell me I was thinking only about myself and not Ma.''

''And how would you feel about that?''

''It wouldn't be true. I could still help out, just like I do. The coach said I could work out with the team two afternoons each week, then practice on my own. Lisa comes Tuesday and Thursday, so they don't really need me. Besides, on those days, all I do is sit around the living room depressed.''

''How come, Sammy?''

''I don't know. There's nothing to do. Sometimes, I think I'm just there to show them I care, to show Ma it matters,'' he blurted out. His mouth dropped open in response to his own words.

''What is it?'' I asked.

''You know, that's what I'm doing. It's like all the other games in my house. I never realized I was doing that. It felt so automatic.'' He laughed self-consciously, then nodded. ''You want to hear something crazy I just remembered? One time I got into the football game on TV and started rooting for the Jets. As soon as I heard someone coming downstairs, I looked away from the set. I can almost remember making sure I looked sad so they'd know and not think the wrong things. Wow!'' He cleared his throat and continued. ''I don't know if they would understand about track. Maybe, if I explained it to them . . . but, but I'm afraid.''

''Afraid of what?''

''What happens if they don't understand?''

''Maybe that would be a nice question for you to answer,'' I said.

He laughed. ''I guess I could go back to hanging around in the living room with a sad face.'' He smiled, shaking his head up and down. ''Bears, you know, that's the first time I laughed in a long time. I guess I didn't think it was okay to laugh while Ma's so sick."

"And now?"

"It's okay. I mean here I am doing it. So what!" He paused, inhaled a deep breath, and said, "Yeah, maybe I could go back to track . . . maybe if I talked to them. Ma could be sick a long time and what's the difference since she's going to get . . . to get better." He looked down in his lap. "That's another thing, Bears, suppose, just suppose, she doesn't get better."

"What about it?"

"She's awful sick, I know it—but nobody really talks to me about it. Maybe my father's wrong, maybe the doctors are wrong, maybe they're all lying. That really scares me."

"What about it frightens you?"

Sam squeezed his eyes shut, holding back. "I don't want her to . . . to not be here."

"I understand. But what about that possibility frightens you?"

Sam rose from the bench. He pranced in place like a nervous colt. I stood up beside him and followed as he began to walk.

"She's my mother," he whispered, almost breathless. "Nobody cares about me like her. I need, I . . ." The words became garbled as the tears streamed down his face. "No matter what I do, I'm always, kind of, you know, okay with her. It's not the same with Dad or Sis. Ma and I have something special." Sam stopped walking, bowed his head, and put his hand over his eyes. Silence.

"What are you thinking about?" I asked him.

"Thinking it might be over and she wouldn't be here and I'd be all alone."

"What do you mean, Sammy?"

We began to walk again. Sam watched the seagulls, then peered into my eyes. His mouth moved, but no sound came. He looked away, drew in a deep breath, and began. "Nobody would feel about me the way she does. Dad's into his oscilloscopes. Lisa has her art. Nobody really has time for me except my mother. That's pretty special. I know it sounds silly. I'm al-

70

most seventeen and I have a lot of friends and stuff," he sighed. "I guess I never thought about any of this until she got sick last year. When I was in the sixth grade, Ellen Ringer's mother died. She used to be such a great kid, but ever since then she's different . . . weird, alone. I know she's miserable. Maybe that's what happens."

"Do you believe that?"

A half-smile creased his face. "Not really. There I go again with my 'not really.' Even when everyone said Ellen was a great person, I thought she was weird. Only, I guess, she got weirder." His eyes filled with tears. "I just can't imagine Ma not being here."

"What about her not being here disturbs you?"

"It's not fair."

"In what way?"

"Most people live till they're old, even really old like my grandparents." He paused, then closed his eyes. "I don't think I'd be okay without her."

"Why not, Sammy?"

"Well," Sam said, "if I can't talk to anybody like I do to her, then I'd be more mixed up."

"Do you believe that?"

"Sort of."

"Why?" I asked.

"I don't know. I guess I'd get along, but it doesn't feel like it."

"If you felt okay without her, what do you think that would mean?" I asked.

"That she didn't matter and . . . that I didn't . . . love her enough." Sam shook his head as he flopped down on another bench. "But, Bears, that's not true."

I sat down beside him. "Okay, then what is true?" Sam smiled, but didn't answer. "Why are you smiling, Sammy?"

He peered directly at me. " 'Cause it's like what we talked about before with the track team. Not having fun, feeling bad to show myself and everyone else that I care."

"Could you be happy and still care?"

71

"Yeah," Sam answered in a soft, barely audible voice. "I don't know if that's so easy, but . . . yeah."

As we crossed the meadow to exit the park, Sam told me he wanted to come back and talk more. When we set a date for another session, he nodded his head, tapped my shoulder playfully, then trotted down to the lake. Resting on one knee, Sam Millen faced the animals in the water and made a series of ducklike sounds. After completing a short repertoire, he turned and smiled at me, obviously satisfied with his effort.

The conductor braced himself against a pole as the train lurched noisily around a curve. He waited a calculated eleven seconds until the cars reached the straight track again, then continued his journey down the aisle, pushing his way through the crowded commuter train and clipping the tickets of those he passed. The seven forty-five to Manhattan had always been the most popular run into the city, a fact the trainman tolerated without any humor. When a man puffed smoke into his face, he muttered obscenities while punching holes mindlessly in little two-by-five-inch computerized stubs.

At the end of the car, he folded his hands across his chest and waited impatiently for a response from four men playing cards. These passengers had faced two seats toward each other, spread a newspaper over their laps like a portable table, and immersed themselves in a game of gin rummy. The conductor cleared his throat noisily. The game stopped. Each man delivered his ticket into the trainman's hand, except Chad.

Martin Rebman tapped his friend on the knee.

"Oh, excuse me," Chad said as he held his stub up to be punched.

Once the conductor left, one of the men picked another card from the deck and inserted it slowly within the fan of six others in his hand. A victorious grin curled his lips. He rubbed the tip of his nose for luck, then spoke boisterously.

"Ah-ha! I'll raise a quarter."

"You're on," another man barked as the train began to decrease its speed. He tossed his coin onto the newspaper.

Martin surveyed his cards, then made his own contribution to the kitty.

Chad pushed himself to concentrate. He put his quarter down, threw out two cards, and drew two more from the deck. As he slipped them into his hand, he turned casually to watch the train ease into a suburban station. Chad stared into the expressionless faces of some people waiting on the platform. In the road, by the crossing gates, he noticed a small funeral procession. The voices and noises around him suddenly became muted. Chad wanted to turn away, but, instead, found himself scrutinizing each vehicle, especially the limousine stopped directly behind the hearse. A man, about his own age, sat somberly next to the window. The image blurred, forcing Chad to rub his eyes. When he looked up again, he saw himself sitting in the car with Lisa beside him. He winced, rotated his head away from the window uncomfortably, stared blankly at the other passengers on the train, and tried to suppress the first real panic he had experienced since Vietnam. The muscles in his abdomen knotted. He pressed the cards in his hand so hard that his fingers numbed. Slowly, almost as if he was out of control, his head angled back toward the glass pane beside him. His vision became riveted on a young man in the front seat of the limousine, a young man who appeared to be his son.

"Chad. Hey, Chad," Martin said, "it's your turn."

Startled, he jerked his attention back to the other players. Perspiration bubbles now dotted his forehead. "I'm out," he replied without even looking at his cards. Two of the men eyed him suspiciously, then refocused on the game.

As the train pulled out of the station, Chad forced himself to take the one last look he dreaded. The same strangers he had seen originally in the vehicle were back in place. The young man in the front seat no longer resembled Sam. The funeral procession receded as the morning commuter gained momentum and Chad Millen returned reluctantly to the game.

Sam's body tingled as he stood in line for the school bus. He always delighted in the sensation that he experienced after a rigorous workout, but today the aching muscles felt like a lover's embrace. He had driven himself to the limits of his endurance and his body, though technically "out of training," reconfirmed its natural agility.

The bus lumbered to the curb like an old dinosaur, sputtering fumes and backfiring twice before coming to a final rest. The door snapped open. Several students jostled each other as they squeezed up the steps, though most, obviously content with the ritual, waited their turn patiently. Sam flashed his pass, a requirement for everyone using the last shuttle leaving the school, and made his way down the aisle. A group of boys entered the bus noisily; they called out to Sam.

"Hey, Sam," one yelled. "Good to have you back."

"Thanks," Sam answered.

"Yeah!" added another boy as he made a victory sign with his finger and winked. "The track team needed you, ol' buddy."

A third youngster threw up his arm and cheered, "Haley Oaks, you ain't got a chance now."

A chorus of laughter burst from the group as they slid into their seats. Sam smiled self-consciously. He took a window seat near the rear of the bus and nodded to the unfamiliar student who flopped down beside him.

Sam never needed anyone to tell him he was a good runner; his stopwatch and placements during competitions affirmed his skill. The viewpoints of his teammates had never been articulated, except when they cheered him toward a finish line, a ritual they performed for everyone. But now, off the field, to hear them verbalize their excitement about his contribution astounded him. He had always viewed track as different than the other team sports. A runner always ran alone, no passing of balls or assisting others under a net. As a result, it attracted a different type of participant. Not like smart-assed Hank and Bud, he thought.

Leaning his head against the window as he waited for the bus to depart, Sam detached himself from the surrounding conversations and ignored the mischief brewing among his schoolmates. He watched some students play touch football on the grass near the side of the building. Suddenly, Ginny burst through the school exit door and ran toward the bus with her hair flying and her hands locked in front of an armload of books. A huge, black case with a bulbous bottom hung from her shoulder. Sam followed her movement and smiled; even when she ran, she looked like a swan in flight. As she drew closer to the bus, a husky boy, darting past her, slammed into her by accident and knocked her books out of her arms. He mumbled a quick apology and continued running. Sam watched the papers from her looseleaf fly in all directions. Ginny shook her head and stamped her foot.

Sam bolted from his seat, excused himself to the person beside him, and pushed his way out of the bus while everyone looked on in surprise.

Ginny began picking up the papers from the ground. Sam joined her without comment. After placing his books and the bag holding his track clothes down beside her, he snatched up the papers as quickly as possible from the grass and then ran into the street to retrieve the others. He held his hand up to the bus driver to stop him from moving away and hitting him. Ginny stood still for a moment and watched him admiringly. Finally, they both scanned the grounds one last time for any stray sheets. Success. Not a page in sight.

Sam scooped up his books and track bag, pivoted around and ran toward the bus yelling, ''C'mon, Ginny. Run for the bus!''

Ginny secured the case dangling from her shoulder, then grabbed her books and charged after him.

As they both scurried toward the bus, it began to pull away from the curb. Sam banged on the door. ''Hey, hold it!'' The huge vehicle jerked to a halt; the driver opened its doors begrudgingly. Sam and Ginny climbed in breathlessly and found two places together in the rear section. They flopped into their seats, still panting, and, as they turned to face each other, laughed.

"Thanks," said Ginny. "Thanks a lot."

Sam looked at the pile of papers he had picked up and placed them in her lap.

"What a mess!" she sighed, as she attempted to shuffle the pages into some semblance of order. Suddenly, the bus lurched into a turn and a handful of papers careened out of her hands. They floated over the heads of those sitting in front of her. Hands reached in all directions, plucking papers from the air and passing them back to Ginny. Sam reached down for one sheet which had fallen halfway into his own open case. After removing it, he tried to close the zipper, but couldn't. The mechanism wouldn't budge. He lifted the track bag into his lap for more leverage and struggled with a tiny piece of material caught beneath the metal catch. First he pushed it, then he pulled it. Nothing short of an operation would move this baby, he surmised. He made one last effort, jiggling the zipper furiously in all directions. When he dropped the bag back on the floor, Ginny reached out, grabbed the handle, and balanced the satchel on her knees. She spent a minute exploring the zipper mechanism, jiggled the slide to one side, and then slid the zipper closed with an easy flip of her wrist. They both roared.

"I'm not always a klutz," she giggled.

"I don't always go charging out of buses, you know, especially without my sword," he jested. "Where are you coming from?"

"Orchestra practice. I play the French horn."

"Oh, should have guessed," said Sam. "With that case, it was either a musical instrument or a machine gun."

They smiled at each other.

"And you?" Ginny questioned. Before he could answer, she ventured a guess. "Football!"

Sam laughed. "Not with this body. Track! Yeah, I'm on the track team."

77

Mimicking Sam's previous comment, Ginny said, "Should have guessed."

A refrain of laughter followed.

"You know," Sam confessed, "it feels good . . . laughing, I mean." Ginny smiled. Sam knew she didn't understand, but he didn't care. He thought about his mother. In spite of the laughter, he was sure he loved her.

The salmon-colored broadcloth, which had been stretched over each cornice above the windows, blended perfectly with the curtains. The patterned carpet picked up the same color scheme; even the quilt had been color-coordinated. Two armoires and a long, low bureau occupied most of the available wall space. The bed, with its antique colonial headboard, faced the door. A jewelry case sat on one night table; the phone and two books on the other. Margaret sat up in bed with a third book in her lap. She watched her husband working diligently on a console he had constructed next to the headboard. His hands appeared as strong as ever, she noted; his eyes as intense as the day she had met him.

"It's almost six o'clock," she said. "Sam will be home any minute."

"Perfect timing," Chad bellowed. "I'm done. Now we'll see this baby in action." He crossed the room and peered out the window just in time to see his son approach the driveway. "Okay, Maggie," he whispered as he rubbed his hands together and returned to the console.

After climbing the few steps to the porch, Sam stopped at the front door, and balanced his books on one hip while searching through his pockets for a key to the house.

"All we do is press this little button down—and *voilà!*" Chad said as he pushed his finger against the appropriate mechanism. Maggie smiled.

The front door popped open before Sam could locate his key. He gaped at the handle, which had appeared to turn automatically, then entered the house cautiously. To his added surprise, he found no one lurking behind the door.

"Now press the top of this button," Chad instructed his wife, "and the door closes. Just make sure the person's inside." They both laughed. Chad shouted downstairs to his son. "Sam, up here. In the bedroom."

Several seconds later, Sam entered the room. "Hey, what's going on?"

Margaret smiled and pointed proudly to the new console.

"Daddy made this for me . . . so now I can open the door from up here." Sam watched his father stroke the instrument in almost the same fashion he had seen him stroke the oscilloscope.

"So, what do you think, Sam," Chad asked his son.

"Great!" At least this time, Sam could understand the usefulness of his father's little invention. More importantly, it seemed to make his mother happy.

"Wait'll you see what I have planned next." Chad paused, glancing back and forth between his wife and son. "A robot that can make dinner, clean the house, and drive me to the station." He laughed.

"Nothing like being replaced by a robot," Margaret said weakly, suddenly self-conscious about being in bed.

"Oh, honey. That was a joke. Nothing or nobody could replace you."

"Bad joke, Dad," Sam said matter-of-factly.

Everyone became visibly uncomfortable, especially Chad, who was aghast at his son's outspokenness. Sam took his books and left the room.

"It's okay, Chad," Margaret said. "Don't give it another thought. I know it's a joke." She squeezed her husband's hand, though he continued to sulk as he stood beside the console. Margaret yelled to her son through the opened doorway. "Sam, come here. I want to hear about school."

Sam entered the room hesitantly, then sat on the corner of the bed.

"Lisa was supposed to be here a half hour ago," Chad noted. "That girl . . . she's so unreliable." He walked over to his son and patted him affectionately on the shoulder. "We can rely on you, Sam. Right? You always help out!"

Sam rubbed his fingers together nervously and spoke in a soft, respectful voice.

"Lisa has a long trip from the city, Dad . . . she's just as reliable as I am."

"Hey," Chad snapped, "what is this . . . attack-the-old-man day?"

"No, no, no," Margaret interjected. "Sam's just sticking up for his sister. That's only natural. He didn't mean anything." She looked at her son. "So, how did you do on the English test?"

"Good," he answered, obviously uninvolved.

"Well—come sit next to me and tell me about each class."

"Oh, c'mon Mom. It doesn't matter."

"It certainly does matter . . . to me. I want to know everything that goes on in your life . . . everything."

Sam repositioned himself beside his mother. He looked over at his father, whose face had already become masked by a thin smile. He waited until Chad picked up a half-empty dish and left the room before he began the ritual of describing the events of his day.

10 ഹ

The early morning sunlight gave the quilt on the bed a soft luster as Margaret finished tucking the corners around the bottom of the mattress. As soon as she finished, she dropped down in the lazy-boy chair near the window and sighed from exhaustion. The smallest tasks had the capacity to drain her energy completely. Sometimes the intensity of fatigue made even breathing a chore. Her bones had now begun to hurt in different parts of her body. It didn't make any sense, she thought, bones don't have feelings, not like skin or muscles or organs. Then the memory of breaking her wrist as a child corrected her assumption; she had been in constant pain for almost three days. Okay, bones do hurt. So what! C'mon, Maggie, get on with it, she counseled herself. Today's a special day. The tone of her pronouncement reminded her of her husband.

Balancing carefully on her arms, she lifted herself out of the chair, thankful that her family had already left for the day. In order not to burden them with her increasing difficulties, she'd stay in bed until the front door slammed closed twice each morning—once for Chad, once for Sam. The process would be reversed in the evening. Her husband and son would encounter her propped up neatly against her pillow with a winning smile on her face. At first, she devised such a ritual in order to sustain her status as the ever-cheerful matriarch of the family. But now, the role had become more difficult to maintain. Not a role at all, she admitted, more like a charade. Nevertheless, she refused to quit, though she didn't quite know why.

Dressing myself used to be so darn easy, she recalled as she struggled to get her right arm behind her far enough to catch the sleeve of her blouse. After managing to get the garment on, Margaret stepped into her skirt and shoes. As she buttoned the blouse, she stared at herself in the mirror. Without makeup, she no longer recognized separate elements of her face with the old familiarity. The texture of her skin had changed distinctly, the surface dry and visibly rough. Lines and discoloration beneath her eyes made her nose and forehead appear more prominent.

Margaret slipped into the chair in front of the table and mirror complex which housed her facial paraphernalia and perfumes. The creams, rubbed gently into her face with the tips of her fingers and topped with liquid makeup and under-eye concealer, lightened the dark areas and softened the crevices under the eyes and around her mouth. More comfortable now with the reflection in the mirror, she applied eye shadow and eye liner with demonstrative expertise. The mascara, the rouge, and the lipstick completed the job. You can still look pretty good, she mused, suddenly feeling decidedly more energetic. She didn't have to remind herself that she'd be at the school in only two more hours.

Chad's little digital started to buzz at her from the bathroom. Margaret shook her head, hustled to the medicine cabinet, and threw the switch behind the small, battery-operated unit. Okay, okay, she muttered, not to the clock, but to the absent yet haunting presence of her husband. Supporting herself against the sink, she waited until she caught her breath, then withdrew the vials of pills and downed the appropriate amount from each bottle. Good girl, Maggie, she told herself in a voice similar to the one she used often with *her* kids at St. Dominick's. Her eyes filled with tears. You're a sentimentalist and a fool. She wanted to be strong, yet, admittedly, she no longer fully understood what being strong meant.

What scared Margaret Millen was not that she had changed, but that everything around her had remained exactly the same.

After crossing back through the bedroom, Margaret rested momentarily in a chair beside the small decorative table on the second-floor landing above the entrance foyer. A cane leaned against the wall near her. She stared at the metal tip and remembered clearly the sound of her mother's "third leg" tapping in the corridor as she approached the front door to the apartment after work each evening. She'd understand, Maggie thought, glancing down into the foyer at her own front door and wishing for the impossible. If I could only talk to her for just a minute. A sigh. Her shoulders drooped and her body settled back into the chair.

One of her hands touched the telephone. Margaret hesitated, then let her fingers curl around the phone and lift it. Instead of dialing, she placed the receiver in her lap and studied it thoughtfully. Suddenly, she scooped up the plastic instrument and dialed, then hung up after only the first ring.

"Oh, stop being so silly about this," she said aloud.

Once again, Margaret lifted the receiver and dialed. As the ringing sound gnawed at her ear, she cleared her throat several times.

A sharp click and an exuberant "hello!"

"Hi, Janet," Margaret replied, fiddling with the cord.

"Oh, isn't this something," Janet exclaimed. "I was just thinking about you, Mag . . . and here you are."

"Well, I know, uh, we've both been busy lately . . . but . . ." Margaret disapproved of her own game. Start again, she told herself, and no more apologies this time. Her voice changed, now infused with obvious enthusiasm. "Listen, Jan, Lisa's going to take me to see Eddie and the kids at the school today. Isn't that wonderful? So, I thought, hmmm, maybe you'd like to come too. After all, you've never met Eddie and I know how much you've wanted to meet him . . . God, he's so special."

Janet's voice buzzed into the receiver held at Margaret's ear.

"Oh, isn't that sweet," she said, "but I can't today." A pause. "But, how about next time?"

"Sure," Margaret answered. "Well, have a wonderful day."

"You too, sweetie. Gotta run now—bye." Janet hung up the phone rather abruptly, leaving Margaret holding the receiver and listening to the dial tone.

The old Fiat moved slowly around the curve and eased to a stop at the traffic light. Lisa drove more carefully today than at any time since her state licensing test. She wanted the ride to be easy and comfortable for her mother, whose physical condition frightened her more than she cared to admit. The idea for this outing had been her brainchild for weeks. She made all the arrangements by herself and told Margaret about it only at the last moment. This is what she needs, Lisa thought each time she glanced at her mother sitting in the seat beside her. Despite the obvious frailty, Margaret had a distinctly refreshed and determined expression on her face. She peered out the window at the familiar hedges bordering a large estatelike complex across the road; one more turn and they would be on the school grounds.

The large sign, lettered in a dignified Old English, marked the entrance to St. Dominick's. Margaret giggled as they drove beneath the towering brick arch. Lisa glanced at her quizzically, then scanned the pastoral property unfolding in front of them, suddenly aware of a world she had never seen, a world which had given her mother's life a special meaning over the past eleven years. Evelyn Waller, the school's director, had been only a name. Eddie and the other children were no more than frozen photographs in an album. After witnessing Margaret's little girl glee, she wondered whether she had cheated herself and her mother by not being interested long before now. How do you make up for those incredible gaps? she wondered as she steered the car along the gently winding macadam road that had been lined by tall trees planted over a hundred years ago.

Small fields, carved out between acres of untouched land,

looked like green carpets sheltered by towering evergreens. Each time they passed one, Margaret smiled. These sections had provided her with a place of privacy to take any one of the children when they needed that personal and intimate care difficult to express in a classroom. Not that she had been embarrassed or the slightest bit hesitant. The desire for seclusion usually came from the youngsters themselves, who believed their handicaps and parental abandonment had made them vulnerable enough without their blubbering in public. Crying can be a way of letting go, a way of sharing with others, she once told Alice Foley the day her dog died. Margaret thought of Jessica Townsend, who, after arguing with a classmate, grabbed her hand and pleaded with her to take her to one of the small fields where she then proceeded to scream and curse until her voice gave out. Bobby Green previewed his magic tricks for Maggie there before going back into the building and braving the scrutiny of his classmates.

The car came to a gradual stop in front of a well-kept manor house with vines growing along its aged facade. Margaret took her daughter's hand and squeezed it. Lisa wanted to hug her mother, to tell her how close she felt at that very moment, but, instead, she stopped herself, not wanting to intrude on the visit. This was Maggie's day, not hers, she decided, never considering the possibility that this would be a special day for both of them.

"Okay," Lisa said, jumping out of the car and rushing over to her mother's side.

Margaret opened her door and placed one leg at a time on the ground. She glanced up at the second-story window to what had once been her office.

"Here, Mom." Lisa handed her the cane as she helped her out of the car. Margaret nodded her thanks.

Together, arm in arm, they ambled slowly along a gravel path toward the large, brass entrance door. The cane slipped twice on small stones, though Margaret hardly noticed.

"You nervous?" Lisa asked.

"A little," her mother admitted. She smiled. "It's been a

while." A pause. "I've missed those kids. I hope they remember me."

"Remember you? Some of the team teachers told me you're a topic of discussion for the kids all the time. Eddie asks for you every day. It's the only time he talks."

Margaret's eyes glowed. "Well," she said, leaning toward her daughter playfully, "don't tell your father I said this, but . . . Eddie's quite a little man!"

They both laughed.

Lisa pushed open the front door to the building and held it ajar as her mother made her way slowly inside with the aid of the cane.

"Oh, Margaret," a well-dressed woman with manicured gray hair said as she approached them with outstretched arms. "It's so lovely to see you. Everyone's here, my dear." Evelyn Waller purred a second hello when she turned toward Lisa. "We're pleased you could bring your mother to us, Lisa. So very pleased." She shook both their hands in a gesture that appeared oddly formal in contrast to her words.

As the three women walked down the main corridor, Lisa admired the old wood panels and hand-hewn beams. This isn't a school, it's a fortress, she mused until some bulletin boards in the distance became apparent. Yes, it's a school. The rather bizarre and seemingly inept drawings displayed on those walls gave the students their chance for immortality . . . for a day, a week, a month. Margaret also looked at the framed corkboards searching unsuccessfully for some familiar painting. In her four-month absence, all the pictures had been changed; perhaps, even more than once or twice, she calculated.

As they approached a classroom door, a young boy on crutches came out of the room and stopped short. He flashed a huge grin at Margaret, then reopened the door to the classroom.

"She's here," he yelled inside. "She's coming . . . right now." The little boy turned again and said, "Hi, Maggie. It's great to see you."

The headmistress bent down and spoke to the child firmly. "Mrs. Millen, Robert, not Maggie. Remember?"

"Mrs. Millen," he repeated.

Margaret winked at him, then ruffled his hair. "It's terrific to see you, Robert," she said. "You're doing wonderfully on those crutches, better than I am on this cane."

The youngster noticed her walking stick for the first time.

Evelyn ushered everyone into the classroom. An avalanche of screams and shouts assaulted the group as fifteen students between the ages of ten and thirteen voiced their hellos simultaneously. Some were in wheelchairs, others in leg and arm braces; a few supported themselves on artificial limbs.

Margaret glanced back at Lisa and grinned.

"Maggie, Maggie," one girl yelled while she waved.

"Look, I got a new hand, Maggie," a boy announced, holding up one arm and presenting the shiny metallic hook peeping out of his sleeve.

She waved back to the little girl, then shook the boy's mechanical hand with tremendous excitement on her face. Margaret looked over her shoulder at her daughter and whispered, "Aren't they the greatest?"

Lisa couldn't talk; she could only smile and nod.

Evelyn tapped Maggie's shoulder and pointed to a sign made by the children. Although some of the letters had been rendered clumsily, the message was clear: "We love you, Maggie Millen."

Almost an hour passed before the class settled back into the more normal routine of the day. Margaret tried to respond to all the requests for her assistance, though she glanced often at the youngster at the corner table who had remained aloof from the proceedings. Lisa focused on the same child. Eddie looked just like his picture, she thought as she helped the teacher, her mother's replacement, conduct a simple demonstration in liquid measurement. Most of the students participated, except for Eddie, of course, whose body, propped in a wheelchair, leaned lethargically to one side. Yet, despite the pose, his eyes, accented by the coal-black skin of his face, illuminated an explosive intensity. He stared at Margaret's cane when she walked from desk to desk, but looked down at the floor when she approached. Touching her head to his, she, too, peered at the green tiles. After a couple of seconds, they both laughed.

"So, have you found anyone you'd like to talk to yet?"

Eddie shook his head "no."

Margaret seated herself in front of him, bent across the table and looked directly into his eyes. She stroked his arms. "I'm so happy to see you," she whispered. "Tell me how you're doing."

"I've been working real hard on our card game."

"Have you!" Margaret exclaimed. "Well, you know, once you've got it really good, you're going to have to find somebody to play with."

"I'll play with you," he said emphatically.

"Well, sure, but if I'm not here . . ." She paused, not quite knowing how to complete the sentence.

"Are you sick?" asked Eddie.

"Yes—yes I am."

"Very sick?"

Margaret stared into that little face and marveled at his question. No one had ever asked her that before.

"You know, Eddie, we've always been honest with each other, haven't we?" He nodded affirmatively. "So we wouldn't want to change that now, would we?"

"Nope!" he answered.

"I'm very sick," she declared. A pause. "But I'm working on getting better." An awkward grin fluttered across her face. "Hey," Margaret began in a completely different voice, "don't think you can get away with not playing cards with me today. Now, where are they?"

Although Eddie's fingers curled up uncontrollably, he reached into his lap and pressed both hands around a deck of cards. Very carefully, he lifted them onto his wheelchair tray, then slid them onto the table. In another maneuver, he dumped the cards out of the box and pushed five cards to Margaret using the back part of his thumbs.

"Okay!" she blurted in obvious approval of his increasing skill; then she twisted her hands like his and tried to push one card at a time into the spaces between her fingers. Margaret managed to squeeze the six of diamonds and queen of hearts between her knuckles and the first joint of her fingers, but kept dropping the others and laughing each time she did.

"Oh, do I need practice. I used to be better, wasn't I?"

"You just weren't born with the right equipment, Maggie," he quipped, displaying his cards which he had wedged neatly between his knuckles. Eddie began to giggle.

Margaret furrowed her forehead as she concentrated, dropped another card, and began to laugh too.

Their game progressed very slowly. Instead of breaking for lunch, they remained at the rear table, thoroughly immersed in each move. Lisa served them sandwiches from the lunchroom. Eddie told her that he liked her too, that if Maggie couldn't come too often, he would talk to her. Lisa squeezed his shoulder, glanced at her mother admiringly, then withdrew from the room quietly.

Two hours later, after packing the cards back into the box, Margaret rose from her chair. "Next time I'll beat you." She bent down, kissed him on the forehead, and whispered, "You, my little man, have given me the greatest thing you can give anyone . . . yourself. Nobody can ever take that from me, can they?"

With the aid of her cane, she walked away from him very slowly. Margaret gave in to the urge to stop and look back. Eddie, his eyes glazed, waved one curled-up hand. She curled her hand, like his, and waved back.

As the car pulled away from the school, Margaret Millen tried to freeze the images of the children's faces in her mind, holding onto them desperately so that they would never fade.

Lisa shifted into second gear and exhaled noisily. "I didn't realize . . ." she said to her mother. "I never understood until today."

Chad stood alone at the bay window, consumed by his silent vigil. Thirty minutes had passed since his arrival from work. He spent most of that time looking into the street, his eyes scanning a distant corner like a disciplined sentry. His fingers tapped nervously against his legs, his face somber and fixed. Chad didn't move or flex a single muscle when Lisa's car drove into the driveway, nor did he volunteer any assistance when his daughter helped his wife from the vehicle. Margaret appeared utterly exhausted, although a peculiar grin adorned her face.

As the two women walked very slowly toward the front door, Margaret said, "He didn't even bat an eye—just beat me at every hand."

They laughed.

"And what about tiny Stephanie, who came over later and wanted to place bets . . . three-to-one on Eddie."

More laughter. They locked arms as they climbed the steps. Suddenly, the door flew open. Chad greeted their cackling with a forced smile.

"Oh Chad . . . you're home? We had such an exciting day at St. Dominick's, didn't we, Lisa?"

"We sure did, Mom," she replied. "It was beautiful."

Chad put his arm firmly around his wife and guided her to the stairs. He looked back at Lisa, a sudden anger oozing from his eyes. She recoiled instinctively.

"I'm going to get undressed and take a little snooze," Margaret said. "I'll tell you all about everything later, Chad."

"Sure, honey," he answered.

Margaret climbed the steps very slowly. When Chad tried to help, she motioned to him that she could do it by herself. He acceded to her wish, but, nevertheless, positioned himself beneath her on the staircase as a protective measure. After his wife disappeared into the bedroom, he turned and stared at his daughter. At that very moment, Sam entered through the front door.

"Hi, folks. Lisa, how come you're here?"

Nobody answered. Chad came down the staircase and walked solemnly across the foyer into the kitchen. Lisa, still dumfounded by his attitude, followed him.

After removing a glass from the cabinet, Chad filled it with water from the tap. Sam stood at the doorway to the room and looked back and forth from his father to his sister.

"What's the matter, Dad?" Lisa asked.

"What's the matter?" he sneered in a furious, yet controlled manner. "You have some nerve, young lady. You just take it upon yourself to go gallivanting around with your mother . . ." His voice quivered. "She could have been seriously hurt. She could break a leg, just like that." He snapped his fingers to accent his point. "She's weak; her bones are very brittle . . . don't you understand?"

"No, Dad," Lisa hissed, "I don't understand."

"Well, you never do."

"You know," she added, "I'm really tired of the way you treat me. I don't think this has anything to do with Mom. No matter what I do, I'm no good. You're just a . . ."

Chad cut her off by throwing the remainder of the water in his glass at her face.

"Dad!" Sam exclaimed.

Lisa backed away from her father. Her hands, which remained at her sides, were clenched into fists. "You're crazy," she screamed. "You know that . . . you're fucking crazy." Lisa spun around and stormed past her brother. Chad started to lift his hand up, but dropped it when he heard the front door slam shut.

Sam's mouth hung ajar. He watched his father for a couple of seconds more, then backed out of the room.

11 🐎

My second session with Sam Millen began early in the morning, just after the sun had crept over a distant building. The dew wet the lawn beneath my sneakers as I walked toward the black cinder track. The school building and athletic fields, alive with students during the day, were deserted at this early hour. A cool, brisk wind pushed the clouds rapidly along the horizon.

Sam had phoned two days before, requesting this as the site for his next session. He convinced me quite easily, since I usually jogged several times each week. He called it a celebration. After what he characterized as an easy discussion with his parents, he had visited his coach and rejoined the team.

Stepping in front of the bleachers, I peered at a sunbleached runner moving gracefully into the far turn. His legs glided out easily from beneath his athletic form, touching the ground so lightly, so silently, that I questioned my vision.

Then a familiar voice bellowed across the field. "Hey, Bears."

"Hey, Sam," I shouted back. If we were both on schedule, as planned, he would be finishing his seventh mile. We would do the last three together.

"Number seven going down," he affirmed. "Start and I'll catch up."

After taking three deep, cleansing breaths, I leaned forward slightly to generate the initial thrust, pushing off with my toes until the motion of my legs began to carry me. The wind filled my lungs with an invigorating coolness. It whipped through my hair and made my eyes tear. As I rounded the first turn, Sam came alongside. No strained face. No panting chest. He seemed perfectly relaxed, like a casual stroller, his long, limber strides awesome in their ease.

"You're serious about this, right?" I asked.

Sam stared at me for an instant as if surprised by my presence, then looked back down at the track as he spoke. "If you can ask the questions, I can answer them," Sam assured me. "The wind works against you on this side, but it'll carry you on the way back. Fall into it with your body—it'll help."

"Will do," I acknowledged. "Whenever you're ready, Sam, start talking. I'll let you know if I'm going to keel over."

We both laughed.

Suddenly, Sam became very solemn. "Everything seems to be falling apart . . ."

"What do you mean?" I asked.

"Like my dad . . . and Lisa." He paused. "Bears, do we always have to talk about unhappy things?"

"Well, no, we don't. But, maybe, if you come to understand those 'unhappy' things, you'll be more comfortable and, as a result, clearer in handling them."

Sam nodded. "Yeah, like last week with track. You know, both my parents really understood about the team. What a surprise! In fact, they called it a mature move . . . get that—mature move," he repeated, delighted with the words. "Everybody on the team has been so nice. I really missed it."

We ran for almost a minute in silence, then Sam spoke again. "You know, sometimes I think I made the whole thing up . . . that stuff about a special relationship with Ma. I want to do what's right!"

"What do you mean, Sammy?"

"I want to care. Sometimes, it's a pain to help her all the time and I feel awful when I think it's a pain."

"Why?"

" 'Cause if I was a good son," he said, "I wouldn't think those kinds of things."

"Do you believe that?"

"Well, my father never complains, and neither does Lisa. At least they never tell me. When I think about staying with the guys and playing some ball after school, I feel horrible."

"Why?" I asked.

" 'Cause I shouldn't think about those things, at least not now."

"Why not?"

He drew in a deep breath; for the first time his running cadence became tight. "Everybody in the house is counting on me to do my share."

"What are you afraid would happen if you didn't feel bad about those kinds of thoughts . . . like staying after school?" I queried.

"That maybe I'd think about them more often and maybe I'd stay," he declared.

"Do you believe that?"

"Well . . . no, not really. I wouldn't stay; I'd probably go home."

"Okay, then do you still see those thoughts as bad?"

"I guess they're okay. I kept thinking they'd mean that I'd suddenly decide not to help. You know what, I just decided your questions aren't so weird after all." He paused, rubbed his eyes, and sighed. "Bears, do you think it's okay to sometimes feel helping with Ma is a pain?"

"If I told you what I thought, Sammy, I'd just be telling you about my beliefs and my reasons. It wouldn't really help you focus on what you believe. So maybe, it'd be more productive if you answered the questions. Is it okay to see helping out as a pain?"

"This morning it wasn't—now, well, it's okay. I could still care and sometimes think that."

"Sammy, what does the word 'pain' mean?"

He smiled. "When I don't want to do it, I call it a pain. Silly, huh? I guess if you said it wasn't okay to do that, then I wouldn't know what to think.''

"Why, Sammy?"

"Because, maybe," he said, purposely avoiding my eyes, "maybe, I'm only being selfish."

"Are you?"

"In a way," he answered. "Everybody else just thinks about Mom all the time. With me, it's different."

"Let's talk about your observation. Unless you can crawl inside someone else's head, you can't really know what they're thinking all the time. Maybe your father and sister think about your mom all the time, maybe not. But you can never be sure of either conclusion," I said, allowing a lapse of several seconds before I continued. "For the moment, let's assume your assessment is correct . . . they only think about your mother and you are different, you think about other things as well. What's selfish about that?"

"I'm only thinking about me, things that are important to me. When I'm with my mom, it's different."

"What do you mean?"

"When I'm with her," he asserted, "I'm there for her, not me."

"How's that?"

"Well, I help her get things, make her tea. Sometimes, when she's tired, I feed her like she used to feed me when I was sick."

"Okay, you help her when you are there, you do things to make it easier for her. But why are you there?"

"To do that, to make things easier for her. That's what I want to do."

"Why do you want to do that?" I asked.

"There's no answer," he insisted. "I just want to do it, Bears."

"Maybe if you can guess at an answer, something will come. Try it. Listen to the question again. Why do you want to help make things easier for your mother?"

"For her and, if I guessed, I'd say it makes me feel good inside."

"Now that you've said that, does it sound true for you?"

"Yes," he smiled.

"So then a reason for doing it is the good feelings you get inside. If you didn't get that good feeling, do you think you'd want to do it?"

"Probably not," he answered. "I'd still do it, but I don't think I'd want to."

"So are you saying you want to?"

"Uh-huh."

"Then if you want to and you get this good feeling, are you there for you?"

He nodded. "Yeah, but I never realized that before. Somehow it all got mixed up. I always thought when you are there for yourself, that's selfish, that's bad, but I guess you're always there for yourself in some way. That's incredible! I really understand a lot more now. But what about staying after school?"

"What about it? Is it okay to want to stay with your friends after school?"

"Yeah!" he replied. "Definitely. But you know what, I still want to go home and help out some more. Funny, I was afraid, deep down, I really didn't want to help, like I had to and that was the only reason." He nodded his head. "I love my mother. I guess I don't use that word too often out there. It's nice to know I love her and still can think about going back to the track team. I'm going to try."

"To try for what?" I asked in a voice somewhat thinner as we began the third mile together.

"To help out at home," he affirmed, "and, at the same time, train with the team on my free afternoons. I know I'm smiling, Bears. I feel good about what we talked about, but there's things I didn't say." He shuddered.

"Well," I replied, "if we didn't get to them today, we can try again next week . . . or the week after . . . but only if you want to."

"I do," Sam said. "Yes, I do." He smiled again.

The old three-story building, a converted Victorian, stood among other similar structures. Several elderly people occupied chairs on the huge, wraparound porch. Two groups gathered around portable tables, engrossed in their respective card games. A silver-haired lady, assisted by a nurse, entered through the front door as several young people exited noisily. Although a large, wooden plaque identified the Senior Citizens' Center, the colors of the building itself served as a rather demonstrative sign. In contrast to its neighbors, which had been painted in subdued coordinated colors, the SCC had been doused in a lively sky blue with orange trim and yellow doors.

Charles Millen, kneeling on the ground beside the porch railing, looked up admiringly at the structure for a few seconds. He had hand-picked the colors himself. Each had been chosen with a particular rationale: the blue represented the sky; orange and yellow symbolized the sun. When some members complained about his choice, he told them it was just like being in Florida with blue skies and a hot sun all the time. To his amazement, the explanation satisfied most of his opponents. He laughed at his own sophistry, then hammered a nail expertly through a post beneath the railing. He wouldn't trade the power in his hands for all the words in the world. Charlie promised himself that, unlike his peers who had already retired to their rocking chairs, he would take his last breath standing tall.

A young volunteer stepped out onto the porch, carrying a glass of juice in her hand. She peered at the two groups playing cards, then scanned the others seated against the back wall. "Mrs. Kramer?" she called, now searching in the opposite direction. Nobody answered. "Mrs. Kramer!"

"Leave it with me, Barbara," Charlie said, pinching his hat in the center and lifting it a fraction off his head in what became an absurd greeting. The fact that the brim had been turned backward did not appear to disturb him. "I'll find her."

The woman looked at him pensively for a moment, hesitated, then handed the glass to him. The old man put his hammer down on the ground, stood up, and walked around to the side of the building. He knocked on the door of a seemingly empty blue van.

"Mrs. Kramer, your juice is here," he said softly.

A tiny voice responded. "There's no one here."

"Of course," Charlie corrected himself. "Well, do you think 'no one' would like some juice."

Suddenly, a small hand reached out through an opened window. "Don't look!" she said.

"Do I ever?" Charlie asked. No response. He shielded his eyes and deposited the glass into her waiting hand. Returning to the front of the center, he picked up his tools, moved several feet, and began testing the strength of other posts. When he located one that moved, he reinforced it, top and bottom, with nails, then dabbed the area with touch-up paint. After completing a small section, Charlie stood up to evaluate his work from a slight distance. He hummed a jazzed-up version of "Five-Foot-Two" and kicked his heels together, almost imperceptibly, as punctuation. Yup. Ain't a soul could do better than that, he thought, and then continued with his work.

Sam, still dressed in his running gear, walked across the lawn in front of the SCC building and scrutinized the area, locating his grandfather immediately. Instead of approaching him, he stopped and listened to his singing. Sam wondered if his grandfather had always been so happy or was that something that came with years. He seated himself beside the old man, but Charlie didn't notice him. Finally, Sam took the paint can and brush and painted an area immediately after Charlie completed a minor repair. The old man whipped around, folded his arms, and then smiled broadly.

Sam shrugged his shoulders and grinned. Charlie nodded. They worked together in silence for a couple of minutes.

"I just wanted to be with you, Grandpa," Sam said. A few more seconds passed. "Thanks for the sessions with Bears."

Charlie smiled, but didn't answer. Instead, he pointed to another spot which needed paint. Sam covered it quickly, displaying the same diligence as his grandfather.

"How's Grandma?" he asked.

"You know Grandma," Charlie replied. "Running around acting as if everything matters."

"Doesn't it?"

Charlie laughed. After a moment, Sam laughed too, though he didn't know why.

"So," his grandfather declared as he buried another nail into the railing, "you suddenly got a calling to be with us old fogies, huh, Sammy-my-boy!"

"No—just with one old fogy."

Charlie nodded. He liked Sam's answer. "Well, then," he said, pointing to the post he had just secured to the base of the porch, "get to it."

Sam applied the paint carefully. "I love you, Grandpa."

Charlie Millen stopped working. He looked back over his shoulder at his grandson. He eyes became glazed. He tapped the boy's leg gently, then continued driving nails into the loose posts.

The two of them labored together for hours. By late afternoon, they had completed repairing the entire perimeter of the porch. Charlie hammered the last few nails. As Sam waited, brush in hand, for his grandfather to finish, he noticed a pair of legs beside his head. He looked up, surprised at the identity of the person towering over him.

"The football player," Ginny said, barely containing the wide-eyed smirk plastered across her face.

Sam puffed out his chest, trying to fulfill the image momentarily, but, then exhaled self-consciously.

"John Philip Sousa's great granddaughter, I presume," he countered, recovering quickly from his initial awkwardness.

Ginny squatted and peered at the railing. Just as she began to talk, so did Sam.

"What are you doing here?" he asked.

"How come you're working . . ." she began, interrupting herself as their words overlapped. They both laughed.

Sam tapped his grandfather and said, "Do you know Ginny . . . Ginny French Horn?"

Charlie smiled politely at her as he put his tools in a small red carrying case. "The names these days. What happened to the good old ones like Jones and Adams?"

He pointed to the last nail heads. "C'mon, Sammy, you got a couple more to do." As his grandson did the final touch-up, the old man mumbled aloud. "Ginny French Horn?" He glanced at the girl. "Ah, don't mind me, little lady, you got a wonderful name . . . an original."

Charlie pulled Sam to the side and whispered through his teeth like an undercover agent. "That's not her name, Sammy. It's Ginny McKinley." He nodded confidently. "Better keep your eye on that one."

"I will, Grandpa," Sam replied. "I promise." He smiled across at Ginny.

It was not difficult for Sam to offer to escort her home. After saying good-bye to his grandfather, he guided Ginny through a narrow alley which opened onto a busy boulevard lined with massive department stores and shopping arcades. They walked leisurely together, the initial portion of their journey punctuated by silence. Finally, Ginny spoke.

"I only give one Saturday a month, but I love it," she said. "Old people are kind of special."

"I always thought Gramps was off the wall," Sam admitted, "but maybe it's everyone else."

Ginny cocked her head to the side and eyed him quizzically. As they passed in front of a drugstore, Sam took her hand. "In here. I just have to pick up a prescription for my mom."

They waited at the counter for several minutes. A man, dressed in a green tunic, typed a label. "One more second," he bellowed, waving to Sam and smiling at Ginny.

"What's wrong with your mom," she asked.

"Some kind of anemia," he replied.

Ginny smiled sadly. "You're lucky."

Sam stared at her. He might have asked her a question, but the pharmacist distracted him. "Just sign it here, Sam," the man said, holding out a charge pad. He signed the slip and took the vial of pills.

As they left the pharmacy, Sam noticed that Ginny still had that peculiar melancholy expression on her face. The pain he thought he saw in her eyes scared him.

"My dad was sick two years ago," Ginny began, responding more to her inner need to talk than to any implicit question on Sam's face, ". . . and he died."

Sam gaped at her. Every muscle in his body tensed. He knew he didn't want her to talk about it. Jesus, her father died, really died.

"The doctor said . . ."

Sam interrupted her sentence abruptly. "Ginny, I can't walk you home today . . . not today. I have to go now." Without waiting for a response, he twirled around and walked speedily in the opposite direction. Ginny's face flushed as she watched him cross the street and disappear among the people on the sidewalk.

Although more paraphernalia, such as some books and a neat pile of magazines, occupied the surface of the bureau, the tidiness in the master bedroom of the Millen home was still apparent. The polished facade of the twin armoires, the staccato clicking of an antique clock encased in a glass enclosure, and the soft glow from teardrop lampshades hanging above each night table suggested a certain permanence and predictability for the occupants of the room.

No one in the Millen family would acknowledge, at least out loud, that anything had changed. And yet, even the casual visitor couldn't help but notice the distinct medicinal odor which perfumed every object in the bedroom. Scratches and a thin hiss marred the *Peer Gynt Suite* recording which Margaret had played over and over again. The flowers, which Chad tried to replace once a week, often drooped, their wilted petals sprinkled on the counter top and floor below. The headboard had expanded to include several more knobs and buttons. A new section, still not completed, contained a small panel with a mass of wire rolled into a ball. Two small diagrams had been tacked to the wall behind the bed.

Margaret let her body relax into the mound of pillows piled against the back of the bed. She wet her index finger with the tip of her tongue, held it suspended above her lap for several seconds, then flipped the page of the book sitting in her lap. Although a romance novel set in the seventeenth century would not usually be uppermost in her choice for reading material, the adventure of this feminist story swept her beyond the bedroom. Margaret had never been kidnapped and raped, had never championed over attackers with inexhaustible cunning, and had never beguiled her way into the most fashionable families in northern France. To be immersed in such a contrived adventure five years ago would have been unthinkable. But now she allowed herself to slide deep within the story and cheer for a heroine who survived in spite of overwhelming odds against her.

Chad stood before a full-length mirror in his underwear with a sports jacket on, observing himself and the appearance of the garment. Two other jackets had been draped over the corner of the bed. He touched his abdomen and sucked in his stomach, forcing his chest to expand, then looked self-consciously beyond his reflection to see if Margaret had noticed. She remained immersed in the novel.

Although he never retreated from what he viewed as his responsibilities, Chad had difficulty admitting to any changes he detected in his body. His receding hairline often disturbed him. His fear of becoming a fat, bald, lethargic old man helped him maintain certain standards of diet and exercise. He could respect himself, but there were terms to that respect. And yet his careful scrutiny of his own form never applied to his wife. The fact that Margaret no longer combed her hair into a neat pageboy but merely pulled it off her face and tied it behind her head had not made a significant imprint in his mind. The dark shadows around her eyes had escaped his considered attention since he refused to view her solely in terms of physical attributes and blemishes. But his forgiving nature had little to do with acceptance. What he couldn't see couldn't frighten him.

Once again, he modeled the jacket in front of the mirror. He picked his chin up, then dropped it as if the position of his head influenced his appraisal of the garment.

"Which jacket should I wear, Maggie?" he asked as he faced her.

Margaret looked up and smiled. She turned the book over, carefully maintaining her place.

"Wait," he declared, holding his hand up like a traffic cop. "Before you make up your mind, I'll try each one on for you. Okay?"

She nodded.

Still in his underwear, he removed the sports jacket, hung it over the closet door, then modeled the other two. In each case, he adjusted the coat in front of the mirror, shifted his head position several times, then paraded back and forth in front of the bed.

"Well," Margaret said, "I have to say I'm partial to the blue one."

"Why?" Chad asked.

An easy smile rippled across her face. " 'Cause that's the one you wore for our twentieth anniversary . . . and you looked *magnifique*." She touched her fingertips to puckered lips and complimented him with a very French gesture. Margaret giggled; she had borrowed some of the affectations of the character in her book.

"The blue one it is!" Chad said. He walked around the bed and sat beside his wife. "I still don't feel right going to this dinner party without you, honey."

"There's a first time for everything," Margaret said gallantly. "It's good for your business. Besides, it's only fair to give some other women a chance at something good. Right?" She winked, still playing the character who had conquered the French noblemen.

"Oh, Mag," Chad bellowed a bit too loudly as he tried to join the game. "I bet you just want to get rid of me hanging around all the time."

"You're right," she quipped. "I have a superhero stashed away in the closet."

They smiled at each other awkwardly, then embraced.

* * *

After dressing, adjusting his tie and putting the television on for Margaret, Chad left the bedroom, though he had difficulty leaving the house. He emptied the dishwasher, then removed and dried pots from the counter top and put them in their respective cabinets. Sorting the silverware took another few minutes. Folding towels from the clothes dryer provided him with yet another detour. Get moving, he told himself finally as he walked through the foyer toward the front door. For a moment, he stopped by the oak banister and looked up at the half-ajar bedroom door. Could he go back upstairs and forget the party? he wondered.

Chad never answered the question. One of the watercolors on the wall caught his attention. Apparently, someone had brushed by it, knocking it off-center. He angled the top of the frame, making sure it was exactly parallel to the molding above it, and then walked out the door.

The highway had only a few vehicles roaring over its cement floor, enabling Chad to set the cruise control switch on the steering column for fifty-five and stay in the middle lane. He stared at the broken pattern of white stripes whizzing by and, occasionally, glanced into his rearview mirror. The drone of the engine hummed incessantly in his ears. His eyelids became heavy, his mood somber. He looked beyond the beam of his headlights and gawked at the darkness enshrouding the road. "Why isn't Margaret with me?" he shouted. The intensity of his own voice and the absurdity of talking to nobody startled him. He wondered whether senility was a genetic trait—whether he and his father, indeed, had more in common than he cared to admit.

As the road snaked its way around the reservoir, Chad watched the changing reflections of the headlights skip along the surface of the water and thought of the Maine coastline sixteen years ago.

A much younger Chad and Margaret climbed out on a rocky jetty with waves breaking all around them.

"C'mon, Chad," she called to him, laughing as she led the

way. "You're supposed to be the athlete in this family, not me."

He remembered how agile she was, jumping from rock to rock without the slightest hesitation. She screeched joyfully as the spray from a wave hit her face. When a second wave broke on the rocks and drenched her, she sat, fully dressed, in a puddle amid the rocks and laughed.

A horn, blaring from behind, obliterated the memory. Chad's car had begun to straddle two lanes. He glanced in the rearview mirror, then readjusted his vehicle's path. A truck sped past him, its driver hitting the horn a second time to record his displeasure. Chad looked into the mirror again. This time he stared at his own eyes as they filled with tears. Suddenly, nothing about his face looked familiar. He shook himself, coughed self-consciously, and flipped on the radio. Disengaging the speed control, he concentrated all his attention on driving.

At the party, the intrusion of others helped center him. Erik had come with Janet. Chad thought it peculiar that she never asked about Margaret. Since the Wiltons, who hosted the gathering, knew he would be coming alone, they didn't ask about his wife either. Not talking about Margaret felt more disturbing to him than talking about her. When several guests finally did inquire, he rambled on about her progress and increasing strength. Everyone nodded their satisfaction with his report; even Chad felt bolstered by his own words.

When Ken Ridgefield offered him a drink, he accepted graciously.

"Listen, Chad, I know this is no time for business, but we're having some trouble with the reconditioned scopes you shipped us last month."

"C'mon, Ken, you know they're thoroughly updated, inspected head to toe . . . they're so systematically rebuilt that you damn near can't distinguish them from new."

"Well, not so with this batch." He raised his glass in a mock salute and smiled. "I would say they're suffering from a little combat fatigue."

106

"Impossible!" Chad countered. The intensity of his voice amazed Ridgefield, who forced a smile.

"Chad, is this your first or fifth drink?"

Chad grabbed him by the shoulder. "If there's something wrong with those scopes, we'll fix them," he shouted. A couple near him turned around. Several other guests looked in his direction. "We build them to stand up against anything," he insisted, his voice still considerably above conversation level, ". . . they come through, you hear me."

Ken Ridgefield eased out from beneath Chad's powerful grip. "Yeah, I hear you."

Suddenly Erik inserted himself between the two men. "Hey, Chad, I think it's time we turned to lighter matters . . . remember, this is a party."

Chad Millen stared at him as if he had been lost. "Sure. Okay. You're right." He eyed Ridgefield. "Listen, Ken, you ship them back Monday, the whole lot, and I'll handle them personally. When I finish with each one, everything will be letter perfect."

"C'mon," Erik counseled, pulling his friend.

"Letter perfect," Chad insisted, nodding his head self-confidently. "That's a promise. My personal guarantee." He straightened his jacket and adjusted his tie in the same manner he had when modeling for Margaret. The other man stared at him, but didn't respond.

Margaret sat up in bed, her eyes fixed and slightly glazed. The television had bombarded her into submission, assaulting her with a kaleidoscope of images and, then, when her retinas ached from the electronic assault, the little machine danced a series of commercial messages across its screen, flickering them as patterns of light along her optic nerve and burying them, finally, somewhere in the recesses of her mind. The process numbed her; even her limbs had stiffened.

In a very gentle motion, she twisted her body from left to right. Soon, the increasing pains in her shoulder and at the base of her head forced her to stop. Margaret tried to imagine Chad at the party alone. He'll take care of himself, she thought; he always does. One day there will be another woman on his arm. It's not fair, Chad! If I only had your courage, your strength. Why am I so selfish? She eyed the portrait on the bureau—her and her husband posing before a tennis match. Turning the clock back seemed like such an impossible ordeal, yet Margaret Millen tried to recapture events that had already slipped through her fingers. All she had was the past now and if she lost that, she told herself, she would have nothing. Margaret searched the corridors of her memory for the day the photograph of her and Chad had been snapped. Desperately, she scanned old billboards like a drug addict looking for an angry fix. Faces. Hands. Buildings. A disconnected smile. Laughter. A ball bouncing off a racket. The images raced across an internal movie screen like jumbled elements of a puzzle. Finally, the maze of impressions quivered, then faded from her grasp.

Margaret grabbed the remote control unit off the night table and switched from station to station with no apparent interest. The circular dial rotated through its sequence of channels four times. A throaty sigh whistled through her larynx. Eventually, she hit the "off" button and tossed the gadget to the other side of the bed. Her fingers massaged the muscles in her neck. Her arms flexed in response to various aches.

Suddenly, her body doubled over as a sharp pain cut through her abdominal cavity. Though it passed within seconds, Margaret reached for a pill and the glass of water waiting for her on the table beside the bed. She downed the capsule and first gulp mindlessly, then ran her tongue along the outer edge of her chapped lips. Her eyes focused hypnotically on the water tumbler in her hand. She resisted the first signs of light-headedness, refusing to support her body against the headboard. Instead, she tightened her grip on the glass, but in spite of the effort, her vision blurred and the dizziness overtook her.

In the next moment, Margaret fell forward. Instead of losing consciousness, she became submerged in a remembered image so vivid and so alive that the past and present became indistinguishable. She held a champagne glass in her hand.

108

Chad, Janet, and Erik were also holding up glasses. Everyone laughed. Maggie's hair fluttered in the night wind. From the upper deck of the ferry, lower Manhattan stretched out before them like a jeweled painting.

"To the next twenty years," Erik toasted.

"Twenty?" Chad protested. "I won't settle for any less than fifty. Right, Maggie, at least fifty?"

She smiled at her husband and touched the tip of her glass to his. Suddenly, the champagne began to swirl, drawing her into a whirlpool of foam and bubbles. Margaret tried to stop herself from falling forward, but couldn't.

Her vision cleared abruptly as her upper torso hung limply over her legs. The water had spilled all over the bed. She pushed herself upright with her hands. Her eyes scanned the room. Everything came into sharp focus. And then she remembered the dizziness, the champagne, and the New York skyline. Fifty years, she thought. He said he wouldn't settle for anything less than fifty years. And neither will I.

Riding the high of a sudden burst of energy, Margaret slipped off the bed and marched into the bathroom to get a towel. By the time she walked the twenty feet in both directions, her chest heaved. She tried to control the panting by doing a round of circular breathing that she had once learned in yoga class. Her respiration slowed almost immediately. Nevertheless, the rapid increase in her pulse rate had given her an instant headache. She ignored the pain, mopped up the water, and hummed a section from Grieg's dance suite.

Six-story columns loomed over the marble steps like sleek prehistoric warriors frozen in stone. Sculptural landscapes in bas-reliefs decorated the brocaded roofline. Two mammoth lions, chiseled out of limestone, sat majestically on platforms to the left and right of the entranceway. A midtown bus belched brown clouds of smoke as it jerked to a halt in front of the massive building and opened its doors with a grinding flourish. An old lady with a cane disembarked first, then a mother with two children, a businessman, several students, and, finally, Sam. The city had always intimidated him, but this time, armed with a purpose, he entered its core with a touch more confidence. He glanced down at his notebooks and biology texts. Although he used them in class almost every day, now they would be his props.

His legs carried him easily up the huge staircase and through the soiled, bronze arch. Once in the main lobby, he stopped. A muffled rumble of whispers buried beneath a hushed quiet reminded him of those few moments before a church service.

A group of people, directed by a tall, gaunt man, crossed the corridor in front of him. No one spoke. Several women strolled down another hallway with books in their hands. Their eyes never strayed from the page, even as they maneuvered around corners and through doorways. A little boy darted out from one room and ran into another. Two girls, each with school books tucked under their arms, eyed Sam as they talked and giggled quietly to each other.

Sam extracted a piece of paper from his pocket and matched the handwritten notation with the sign identifying the library's central catalog system. He walked into the three-story chamber and headed toward the far end. Students and individual researchers were scattered around the endless rows of narrow tables on either side of the central aisle. Books lined the walls. A balcony, with ladders and additional shelving, housed periodicals and off-sized journals. Once Sam passed through the card catalog section, he crossed another open expanse, finally arriving at a far corner.

The uniformed man looked up at him lackadaisically.

"Um . . ." Sam mumbled as he withdrew the paper from his pocket again and handed it to the guard.

The officer nodded. "You take the fourth elevator at the end of the corridor, not the third, not the fifth, but the fourth . . . 'cause only the fourth is going to get you where you're going."

"Sure," Sam replied. "The fourth elevator. Got it!"

The man handed him a numbered pass, then pointed his thumb back over his shoulder.

"Thank you," Sam said, moving past the counter and entering a dimly lighted hallway. As he waited for the elevator, he fidgeted with his books. He arched his eyebrows and furrowed his forehead in an attempt to look studious; he even tried squinting in order to approximate the withered expression of someone who typically buries himself in books. The door in front of him opened suddenly, jarring him from his restrained pantomime. Sam entered the fourth elevator as instructed and pressed the appropriate button.

Exiting on the seventh floor, he turned right and stopped to read the signs on each door. Finally, at the end of another darkened corridor, he found the medical section. Sam shouldered the door open. Inside, he encountered a small, heavyset woman dwarfed by her huge sixteen-foot desk. Her arms were buried beneath piles of paper that she collated haphazardly.

"Yes," she said.

Sam flashed the pass the guard had given him.

"Okay, so you found the right room. Have you come to rescue me?" She knew, immediately by Sam's nervous expression that he hadn't understood. "You know, Lancelot rescues Guinevere from this very boring task and they both live happily ever after."

"I can relate," he replied, relaxing his shoulders and smiling. He held up his biology book like a badge and explained that he had to write a term paper on anemia. "And it has to be very accurate, very precise," he assured her.

"Doesn't everything these days," she countered. "Well, young man, you have come to the right place; all you need is good eyes and lots of patience. And no food," she warned, "or we throw you right out. This is a library, not a luncheonette."

"No food," Sam whispered playfully.

"Good," she chirped. "Now that we understand each other, we can begin." The woman unloaded his books and deposited them on a back table.

"My notebook," Sam said, grabbing the small pad from beneath his texts.

"You ready now?"

"Yup."

"You don't need anything else, do you," she quipped.

"No. I'm ready."

"Good." The librarian pulled her glasses toward the bottom of her nose, peered over the top of the frames, and said, "Follow me."

As they moved through the stacks, she loaded book after book into his arms. "And here's Fishbein's for good measure. Ah, and Merck's—a little simplistic, but probably the only one that uses words you'd be able to pronouce." She paused at an oversized volume. "This one has an absolutely delightful section on chronic and degenerative diseases. We'll save it for later, just in case you get bored."

Sam found a corner desk by the window and began his search

through the medical literature. He developed categories of different types of anemia and then listed symptoms under each.

"Transient para-e-the-sis of the upper extremities," he read aloud as he copied the words. "Per-i-ph-eral neuropathy, fatigue, tactile sensations might be impaired . . ."

Two hours later, he returned to the desk, explaining that the symptoms given to him by his teacher did not quite match the ones categorized in the books. To help him further, the librarian directed him to the volume on degenerative diseases that she had omitted on the initial round, then gathered seven journals and piled them on top of his growing stack of books. She admired his determination. Not many students like that anymore, she thought, downing the last bite of a candy bar and waddling back to her desk.

Another hour passed before Sam closed the last text. He waited in line at the front counter, holding all the books and periodicals in his arms. During the past several hours, the stacks had filled with other students, researchers, and interns.

When his turn came, the woman behind the desk stared at him blankly, then grinned. "You were the one doing a bio report on anemia, right?"

Sam nodded his head "yes," but his face reflected his dissatisfaction.

"You didn't get what you want, huh?" she observed as she helped him unload the library books and retrieve his own.

"Not really. There's a couple of symptoms I couldn't find."

"I'm afraid I can't help you on that," the librarian responded. "But wait," she added with sudden enthusiasm. "Professor Borden from the medical college is here. Maybe he can help you find those 'missing' symptons." She smiled. "Just a minute, I'll ask."

A short time later, the woman ushered him into a reading alcove behind the medical section. She pointed to a rather young man in a suit.

Sam hesitated.

"Go ahead," she counseled. "He really knows his stuff."

She patted him on the shoulder, a gesture which reminded him of his mother.

"So you're the detective Mrs. Stiller told me about," Professor Borden said as Sam approached.

"Listen, I'm really grateful, I mean, it's great that you'd help me."

"I can at least try. Let's see your notes."

Sam handed him the pages of data he had amassed.

The two of them reviewed the notes together. Professor Borden rubbed his chin as he looked at the master sheet of symptoms that Sam said his teacher had given him. He compared them with the degenerate signs culled from the literature.

"Your lists are pretty complete," the professor acknowledged. "Brittle bones and coughing are not usually symptoms of anemia, nor are scattered pains in different parts of the body." He paused, peering curiously into Sam's tense face. "I wouldn't worry about it—you got what you need for your report. No teacher in the world will fault you for that."

Sam nodded. "Well, thanks. I really appreciate your time."

The instructor shook his hand and returned to his reading. Sam turned slowly, hesitated, then exited the room.

"Wait a minute," the professor called. "C'mon back."

When Sam entered the reading room a second time, Borden grinned at him, obviously delighted with his current notion.

"There is a disease," he began, "that, initially, is often confused with anemia. It has nearly all the same symptoms, but includes the ones you mentioned that didn't fit." Borden tapped the table top victoriously with his index finger. "That's got to be the disease your instructor wanted you to identify. Pretty slick assignment." He winked at the young man. "Anyway, we got it now; it's called myeloma."

"What's that?" Sam asked.

"Cancer—in the bone marrow. Actually, the worst kind. Terminal. There's no effective treatment, just half measures." The man paused thoughtfully. "The person goes . . ." he added, snapping his fingers theatrically, "just like that, sometimes within a year. Quite a cute number, I'd say!"

114

Startled, Sam backed away, twirled around, and started running. He didn't hear the professor calling after him or see the librarian gaping at his passing form. Sam Millen thought he had wanted to know the truth, but now he cursed it. She won't give in to it, he told himself, she won't!

Powdered white lines divided the cinder track into six lanes. When the buzzer sounded, six boys, already crouched low to the ground, lunged forward, their competition shoes spitting pieces of gravel behind them. A roar bellowed from the crowded bleachers. Students from visiting schools gathered around benches reserved for their teams and cheered.

A tight-lipped coach, his arms crossed belligerently in front of his chest, sneered at Sam Millen with obvious displeasure, despite the fact he had charged into the lead within fifty feet of the starting line. Run with your heart, damn it. This is your race, kid. He never expected the boy to make it on sheer talent. His gangly shape resulted in wasted movements; sometimes his arms twisted outward unnecessarily before pulling forward to properly complement the thrust of his feet. Perhaps in two or three years, when Sam's skeletal structure no longer outpaced the growth of supporting muscles, he would be a polished runner—consistent, predictable, bankable. But what had made the youngster a star among his teammates and peers was his ability to defy his own body limitations and still win. On rare occasions, Sam moved with amazing grace, but, more often, he pushed, twisted, and, ultimately, threw himself across the finish line ahead of the other contenders. The coach never fixated on the boy's erratic style, although, today, his movements had even less regularity than usual. What he detected immediately was Sam's lack of intensity. "Light the fire, Sammy-boy," he shouted, giving vent finally to his own impatience.

Some of the other students began to chant Millen's name as he continued to hold the first position.

"Yahoo . . . go, Sammy, go!" Brian screamed. "You can do it."

115

Ginny, sitting in the bleachers a few seats away, remained silent as she watched. Sam had been so peculiar before the race; he mumbled a curt hello, then passed by her. The thinness of his voice reminded her of the incident in front of the pharmacy. Although she had seen him twice since then, neither of them raised the issue of his abrupt departure.

Some of the fans rose to their feet, blocking her view of the track. Ginny stood up immediately. The runners came into the far turn. "Why is his head down?" she thought. "What's wrong, Sammy?"

The cheering intensified as the competitors neared the finish line. Sam began to lose momentum. Sweat poured like waterfalls down his forehead. He closed his eyes as his hand pressed instinctively against his stomach. Finally, his face began to register pain. He arched forward slightly to compensate as another runner pulled ahead of him and crossed the finish line first. Sam placed second. He walked off the track panting. His fingers rubbed the area just beneath his rib cage.

Ginny watched him move to the side of the field. Brian observed his friend more studiously now. He turned to Ginny, now sharing her concern. They climbed down the bleachers at the same time.

"C'mon, Gin," Brian said as he vaulted over a small fence and jogged after Sam.

As soon as Sam noticed his friend approaching, he removed his hands quickly from his stomach.

"What happened?" Brian asked.

Sam kept walking, offering no response. He looked past his friend and noticed Ginny following for the first time.

"You okay?" she questioned, a little breathless.

He nodded.

Brian eyed Sam's abdomen, held up his hand with a different funny face drawn on it, and ventriloquized in yet another voice.

"If anyone wants my opinion, it's that natural food that

116

tastes like bird seed he's been eating lately. That's causing all the trouble."

Ginny signaled Brian with a facial expression, trying to stop his comedy routine.

"I wish it were that easy," Sam mumbled, changing his direction purposely and walking away. Brian and Ginny watched him leave, then looked at one another dumfounded. Suddenly, Ginny bolted forward and caught up to Sam.

"Were you avoiding me before the race, Sam?"

"No," he said flatly.

They crossed the parking lot together without speaking.

"Have you had these stomach pains a lot?" Ginny asked finally.

"I don't really want to talk about it."

Sam stopped in his tracks and stared down at the ground. Several seconds passed. "I'm sorry, Ginny," he said softly.

She put her hand out and touched his shoulder. "It's all right."

Sam began to walk again. Ginny followed.

"It's not all right," he asserted. "It's not all right!"

They continued their spontaneous hike through two more parking lots, then circled the school building. Their arms touched accidently several times. Finally, Sam reached for her hand and held it firmly. Ginny stared at his long fingers entwined with hers.

"Did the pain go away, Sammy?"

"Yeah," he lied. "Good old runner's cramp. Everybody gets them."

They sat down in the middle of the empty hockey field. Ginny twirled some grass between her fingers. Sam chewed a scallion stalk he had plucked from the ground, then tightened the laces on his running shoes.

"Ginny, do you believe in reincarnation?"

She looked at him thoughtfully. "Well, I don't know." A pause. "Why'd you ask?"

"Oh . . . I was just wondering."

Sam leaned back, folded his arms behind his head and

watched the clouds move across the sky. He considered thanking Ginny for following him, for keeping him company. He thought about holding her hand again. He wanted to tell her about Professor Borden, but couldn't.

The smell of musk perfumed every crevice of the huge loft that Lisa and Jessica had rented. No walls separated one living area from the rest, so the kitchen flowed into the dining foyer, which, in turn, merged haphazardly with the living room and sleeping alcove. Nevertheless, thirty percent of the total footage, particularly portions directly beneath two massive skylights, had been set aside for Lisa's art studio. Two easels, a mammoth drawing board, a life-size papier-mâché rendition of a horse and several tables with small sculptures-in-progress dominated this section.

Jessica sprawled her thin, almost bony, body across an antique Art Deco divan. Her pleated, black pants and bright red, scoop-necked sweater clashed with the faded floral upholstery, which had been worn away at the corners, exposing the old burlap beneath it. For her, strong contrasts were an essential part of good design. Above her hung an old, dark painting of an exotic nymph, partially clothed, with one breast completely exposed and the other quite apparent beneath its silky covering. Much of the portrait had a network of cracks running through it. Jessica liked the cracks and the breasts equally, especially since she had purchased the piece over Lisa's objections. Now, as she munched succulently on an apple and read a back issue of a feminist magazine, she kicked off her five-inch heels and draped her bare feet over the back of the couch, Cleopatra style.

The simple, gray smock Lisa wore had hand prints of paint smeared all over it. Her cotton, drawstring pants had been rolled up to her knees. She had pulled her hair off her face and tied it into a ponytail behind her head. Lisa had worked meticulously all morning on a portrait of her mother. Two photographs of Margaret, taken before her illness, were stapled to the top of the easel. Although the painting had the same soft edges and muted colors apparent in the display of her work at the art show, the specific accents of line and texture made the likeness uncanny in its accuracy. Even Lisa found it surprising. As she detailed the tiny yellow streaks in the iris, she paused. No one would understand, she thought, how incredibly close she felt to her mother when she worked on the portrait. For the first time, she didn't have to squint to see the inner painting.

She stared at her mother's chin and mouth; so many of the features duplicated her own. Jessica had once called the painting a disguised self-portrait, a notion that Lisa had not been willing to entertain. Yet, at times, Lisa did have difficulty distinguishing, in her own mind, between elements of her own face and that of her mother's. Glancing into the familiar, luminous gray-green eyes, she caught a glimpse of herself in the gloss of the paint.

Jessica looked over her shoulder and eyed the painting. "You know, she doesn't look like that any more, Lise."

Lisa stopped momentarily, tightened her grip on the brush, and exhaled noisily. She never turned her head to face Jessie, who shrugged her shoulders casually and continued to read. Her mood disrupted, Lisa stared out the window angrily. Suddenly, she spun around and marched toward Jessica impulsively, the paintbrush still clutched in her hand. When she reached the couch, she bent down and quickly drew a yellow line down the center of the other woman's face.

"You fool," Jessie yelped. "What the hell's your problem? Huh?"

120

Lisa never answered; she swirled theatrically and walked back to her easel. Now she could resume painting.

"Give me some turp, you crazy female. Hurry up before this stuff dries," cried Jessie, still stretched out on the couch. Lisa ignored her.

Just then, a thin, casually dressed man in his early thirties entered the loft. "It's only me," he announced as he strolled through the dining area and approached Jessica.

"Hi, sweetie." A pause. "Oh my lord!" he exclaimed upon noticing her face. "Whatever are you doing, Jess, planning to perform a rain dance or something?" He laughed.

"It's the artist-in-residence gone bats," she snapped. "Do me a favor, Rick, and bring me some turp on a rag, and a sponge, will you?"

Responding to her request, he backtracked into the kitchen and dug through the dishes in the sink. *Voilà!*" he said, holding the sponge delicately between his thumb and index finger. He moistened some paper towels with turpentine as well, then delivered them to Jessica.

"You're a darling," she said. "At least some people around here know how to show a little respect."

"Whoa!" countered Rick, throwing up his hands. "Maybe I'd better depart from these war-torn premises and return after the armistice is signed."

"Naa! Just keep in mind that her creative majesty has her 'period-of-the-brain' today."

"Your claws are showing, Jess," he scolded with a mischievous smile. She growled at him, then reopened the magazine in her lap. Rick crossed the room and stepped over the coffee table, placing himself squarely in the studio section. He studied the painting.

"Hey, Lise, it's quite good. One day I'm going to be able to say, I knew her when . . ." He paused. "By the way, how's she feeling?"

Lisa put the brush down on the lip of the easel and flopped into a nearby beanbag chair. She eyed the painting for a few seconds, then rolled over and faced her admirer.

"You really like it?" she asked.

He approached the easel, nodding his head affirmatively. "Yes, I do. You know, I've never met your mother, yet her face looks so familiar . . . not in these photos so much, but in the portrait you've painted."

"Touché!" cheered Jessica, ready to unearth her pet theory about a disguised self-portrait again.

"Please don't," Lisa said.

"Okay, I'll shut up," she replied, softening her expression.

Lisa withdrew a crumpled pack of cigarettes from her pocket. She tossed one to Jessica, deposited another between her lips, and offered a third to Rick.

"No thanks," he said, throwing her matches from the coffee table.

She smiled at him, then ignited the cigarette and dragged noisily on it. "Hey, Rick, the hypnosis you guys do in psych, any of it aimed at pain control?"

"Absolutely," he answered with a burst of enthusiasm. "That's where it's probably the most effective."

Lisa rolled the cigarette between her fingers. "If . . . if I could, well, arrange it, do you think, I mean, would you work with my mother until she gets over this?"

"I didn't know she was in pain, Lise," he said. "I thought you said she had anemia."

The muscles in Lisa's face tightened noticeably.

Jessica, who had been listening to the conversation, strolled over to the beanbag and waited for the response. When none came, she knelt beside her friend and brushed her fingers affectionately through Lisa's hair. She glanced momentarily at Rick, then slid around until she faced Lisa.

"Did you ever think, Lise, that your father is conning you?"

Lisa recoiled and threw her head back like a young colt. "Why would he do that. Huh? Why?"

Jessie did not answer. She knew she could push Lisa too far and then it would all get out of hand.

"Get off my case, will you!" Lisa hissed. She jumped to her feet, dumped the brushes from the easel into a can, and tossed a sheet over her painting. "Anybody want some apple juice?" No one responded. "Okay, then I'll make us a snack." She flashed a ghoulish clown's face, turned decisively, and marched toward the kitchen.

Jessica and Rick exchanged glances as they watched Lisa's receding figure.

The rush of lunch-hour pedestrians had ebbed. As elevators filled with human cargo in hundreds of skyscrapers, speeding occupants to assigned seats and designated appointments within Manhattan's internal city, Myrna Millen stood alone, outside, at the corner of Fifty-sixth and Third Avenue waiting for her husband. She had glanced at her watch several times in the last minute. The sweep of the second hand annoyed her; time broken down into fractions seemed to inch along, insultingly, at a snail's pace. He's late and getting worse, she concluded. If his life depended on it, he'd still never be on time. And then she saw him. Rather than celebrate his tardy arrival, she shook her head and huffed.

Charles Millen exited the subway staircase with a young woman wearing a full-length peasant dress and a black velvet cape. Her hair had been braided with flowers and thin leather strips. She carried an armful of leaflets and bounced as she walked. At first, Myrna pegged her at twenty-five, but as her husband and the stranger approached, she revised her estimate downward—twenty, nineteen, maybe even sixteen.

"Myrna, the most wonderful thing happened to me waiting for the E train," Charlie announced.

"I can see that," she retorted, avoiding direct eye contact with her husband's companion.

"This is Faith," he said proudly. The girl smiled easily and handed Myrna a brochure from the New Age Fellowship of Light. "You know how I always tell you everything happens for a reason. Well, I missed the train by seconds, ya hear. So there I am, on the platform—no reason to miss the train and suddenly who appears?" Myrna shrugged her shoulders. "I'm surprised at you." He pointed to the girl. "Faith appeared.

Handed me one of those brochures and look." Charlie opened the one in his wife's hand and pointed to the headline which read: "Healing As An Everyday Miracle." He looked at Myrna, and waited for a response. Nothing. "Well," he said finally, "what do you think?"

"What do I think about what?" she asked.

"Humm . . . let me explain," Charlie volunteered. "This young person is a genuine, bona fide healer."

"I'm not a healer, Mr. Millen, I'm . . ."

"Will ya call me Charlie? All my friends call me Charlie."

"Charlie," Faith repeated obediently. "I'm just starting out. We're all healers."

He snapped his fingers. "I'll bet that's true, little lady. We're all healers. How come I didn't think of that?"

"C'mon, Charlie, we still have to get Margaret something."

"But we have." He pointed to the young woman again. "These kids are on to something, Myrna. I can feel it in these old bones." He winked at his companion.

"Perhaps," Faith said in a wispy, lyrical voice, "you'd want to bring your daughter-in-law to one of our circle meetings; it might help. We do a sort of intense group meditation. Anyone who's sick can go into the center and get the light."

"The light?" Myrna repeated.

"Well, that's what we call it."

"Not like a flashlight," Charlie chimed. "Energy. From in here," He pointed to the middle of his chest.

"Oh," Myrna said. "I'm sure you mean well, young lady, but we're a bit old fashioned for that."

"Margaret would love it," he countered.

"Well, I've got to go now," Faith concluded. "Great meeting you, Mr. Mil—I mean, Charlie. You, too, Mrs. Millen."

"You keep up the great work, young lady," he said, taking a pile of pamphlets from her.

The young woman curtsied and left.

Charlie handed a brochure to everyone who crossed his path. As they entered the department store, Myrna knew that if she spoke to him at all, she would scream. Instead of making a scene, she walked silently to the rear of a women's clothing department, trying to appear as if she had nothing to do with the gentleman beside her.

While she rummaged through the bathrobe section, Charlie finished distributing the brochures. He tucked the last one into his breast pocket and rejoined his wife. "Myrna, what are you looking at those for? You already have ten of them."

"It's for Margaret, poor thing."

"Maggie doesn't need a bathrobe, God knows. I can just imagine when it's time for me to leave this world, you'll probably send me off with a whole suitcase full of bathrobes and God-knows-what-else."

"Bite your tongue," Myrna snapped. "Nobody's leaving this world. Talking so crazy lately. I can't hear any more of it!"

"What'd you think of Faith?" he asked as if he didn't hear her previous commentary.

Myrna never answered the question; instead, she pulled a bright yellow robe off the rack and brought it to the counter. Charlie followed her. "Okay, then what do you think about the possibility that we're all healers?"

"I don't think about it, Charlie. I'm trying to help a difficult situation, to make things more comfortable . . . for everyone."

Charlie looked at his wife thoughtfully, then wrapped his arm around her shoulder. "I know," he said softly.

"That will be twenty-one seventy," the cashier barked.

Myrna paid for the garment without comment, but began a whole scenario of directions when the clerk gift-wrapped the robe. Ten minutes later, when she turned to leave, Myrna realized that she was alone again. Now where is he, she muttered. She walked through the women's section, spotting her husband finally atop an exercise bicycle in the sports department. He pumped the wheels vigorously as his eyes scanned the brochure he had stuffed in his pocket.

"I'm done, Charlie," she called.

He hopped off the machine and jogged toward his wife. As

125

they approached the elevators, Charlie flashed the booklet. "Why can't we try it? You could come, too."

She made a clicking sound with her tongue against her teeth. "The doctors know what they're doing. Now hush with this nonsense." Myrna grabbed the brochure, pulled hers from her pocketbook, and ripped both of them into little pieces.

Charlie watched the pieces settle into the ashtray. He looked up at his wife. "I think you're scared, Myrna."

She gaped at him, unable to speak. Regaining her composure, she said, "Maybe it's better to be scared than crazy."

He considered her statement for a second. When the elevator doors opened, Myrna boarded immediately. Charlie just stood there. As the doors closed, he waved to his wife. "Better to be crazy," he concluded.

"Charlie," Myrna yelled as the elevator ascended.

The old man retrieved the pieces of the ripped pamphlets from the ashtray and left the store through another exit. Once in the street, he reassembled the scraps in his hand. An hour later, Charles Millen arrived at the New Age Fellowship of Light. As he waited for the receptionist, he peeked into the meditation room. A huge, pyramid crystal hung from the cathedral ceiling. No chairs. No tables. Piles of pillows lined two walls; thick carpeting blanketed the floor. He nodded his head approvingly despite the fact he knew he would never quite understand. When the receptionist returned, he wrote Margaret's name on a card and asked her if it would be possible to put it in the center of their evening healing circle. The woman smiled and assured him that it would be done. Charlie thanked her and left.

Margaret sat up in bed, propped up by a backrest especially designed for that purpose. Hollows had developed just beneath her cheekbones, making her face appear gaunt and a touch severe. Despite the nagging pain in her back and shoulder, she flipped through a magazine with more interest than usual. Finally, she stopped on a particular page and smiled. "Ah-ha!" she said audibly, turning the magazine upside down carefully so as not to lose her place. Margaret reached into the night table and withdrew a small nail-scissors, a sheet of stationery with a lilac imprinted at the top, a roll of Scotch tape, and a pen.

With precise, economical movements, she cut out a picture of a woman in a tennis outfit, racket-in-hand, and then clipped out a tennis ball. Her skill had a certain surgical finesse. For a wonderful moment, she imagined herself back at St. Dominick's with the kids. Eddie always had a difficult time cutting things out, she remembered, but he could be quite crafty in pasting pieces together. Use whatever strength you have, she'd tell him constantly. Now, Margaret Millen tried to follow her own advice. She folded the paper in half and on the front printed a question in large, black letters:

HOW IS A TENNIS BALL
SIMILAR TO LIFE?

Twisting the tape around her index finger, she made small rolls which she used to fasten the cutout tennis player and ball to the inside page of the card. Below her informal collage, she printed the answer to the question contained on the cover:

THEY BOTH HAVE THEIR
UPS AND DOWNS!

With love,
Maggie

Margaret glanced at the hospital tray beside her bed and eyed the two place settings complete with silverware, sandwiches, drinks, and a bowl of fruit. With difficulty, she shifted her body to the right and reached over the tray, placing her card on top of the farthest sandwich. She smiled, quite pleased with her accomplishment.

After returning the materials to her night table drawer, she picked up a hand mirror and brush. Casually and with minimal interest, she tried to style her hair straight back, finally using her fingers to organize stray strands. Examining the details of her face more closely, she muttered flippantly, "Maybe we could use a bit of color, Mag," and dabbed her cheeks with a rouge brush. "Whew!" she sighed, suddenly fatigued. Margaret dropped her arms and rested her head back onto the pillow with her eyes closed. She remained immobile for a few minutes. Then, with an abrupt jolt, she whipped open her eyes and sat up erect. I'm not giving in to this, she thought. She held up the mirror again for a last check and brushed her hair one final time with a touch more energy. Well, she told herself, that's not much better, but it's something.

The buzzer sounded. Maggie put the mirror and brush down and pressed a button on her ever-expanding console. Janet appeared on the newly installed video monitor, which adjusted its focus and aperture automatically. As she stood at the front door, unaware of being watched, she quickly and nervously pulled off a pair of fancy earrings as well as a matching bracelet and shoved them into her pocketbook.

Margaret observed her silently, then pressed another button and spoke, "Hi, Janet."

Janet looked all around, obviously uncomfortable. The front door opened electronically. Janet spoke to the air. "Maggie, how'd you know it was me?"

"C'mon in, shut the door and come upstairs. I'll show you."

As Janet entered the bedroom, Margaret threw out her arms with a Hollywood flair and said, "Ta-da! Welcome to my boudoir!"

"Well, nothing like push-button living," Janet chirped, eyeing the TV screen and other new additions to the console. "Wait, let me guess."

"Chad," they both said simultaneously. The two friends laughed until Margaret began to cough and hold her chest. Janet backed away uncomfortably. Noticing the other woman's fear, the moment Margaret could speak, she announced, "I've reserved a seat for you." She pointed to the chair on the other side of the hospital tray.

"You know," Janet chimed without looking, "I can't tell you how many times I've wanted to drop over in the last three weeks . . . but, who knows where the time goes."

Half-listening, Margaret said, "I had Chad make us some sandwiches so we can talk and stuff our faces at the same time." She giggled mischievously.

"Oh sweetie, I am so sorry. I should have told you. I have six people coming for dinner tonight—and I haven't prepared a thing yet. I must rush home and do some slaving."

Margaret, somehow, couldn't mention the silly card she made for Janet.

"Look, Maggie, for sure, this weekend. Okay?"

"Sure," Margaret assured her.

Janet went to her friend and kissed her lightly. She hated herself for leaving so abruptly, but she realized that staying would be even more painful. I'm not strong enough, she admitted. I can't watch this happen. I just can't.

"We'll make it this weekend," Janet restated aloud, waving as casually as possible while she left the room. Before exiting the house, she called back to Maggie, "Maybe Erik will be able to come too. Bye, sweetie."

Maggie sat a few seconds staring at the sandwiches. She reached out, took the card, and, without looking, dropped it off the other side of the bed into the garbage pail. A few more seconds passed before she picked up one sandwich, unwrapped it and ate mechanically, one tiny bite after another.

Six oscilloscopes, each displayed on their own pedestal, stood against one wall of the long, rectangular office. Laminated cards tacked behind each instrument detailed their initial production date and specifications. A small, oval conference table occupied the center of the room. Chad sat behind a large oak desk custom inlaid with Formica so that the various metal components he studied would not scratch the wood surface. He flipped through an orderly pile of invoices. From time to time, he hit the buttons on a small electronic calculator built into the base of his phone. The wall behind him contained what appeared to be a huge, smoked mirror, but with the lights in the office properly adjusted, it became a window through which most of the assembly plant below could be viewed. Since Chad's area doubled as a mini-meeting-room, he justified the installation of the two-way mirror as a method of allowing clients to view the automated, final finishing process performed on each oscilloscope. Yet, in point of fact, this surveillance had been his means of ensuring moment-to-moment control over the final assembly of products bearing his name.

Ned Collier, one of the supervisors, entered the office rather frazzled. Despite his white shirt and tie, his hands were stained with grease and oil.

"It's down again on seven," he said.

"That's the third time this month," Chad replied, flipping the switch on the wall beside him as he swiveled around in his chair. As the room darkened, the bench sections of the plant came into view. About twenty people sat idle on either side of a long, narrow table marked with the number seven. The conveyor belt had become inoperable.

The muscles in Chad's jaw flexed as he surveyed the situation. He sighed noisily. "Get Petie. Tell him I want a manual override in place within the hour."

"I don't know," Ned said. A slight quiver in his voice had become audible. "Even if we could figure something out, who's going to crank a conveyor belt all day."

"There's ninety-seven people down there," Chad replied quietly. He spun his chair again and hit the light switch. "Divide it up into ten- or fifteen-minute segments. Everybody will take a turn at it, including you and me. When Petie has it set in place, buzz me . . . I'll take the first shift."

"Suppose he can't disconnect the motor without disturbing the other belts."

Chad rubbed his forehead. "Do a jump with the C-14 overrides we got from Fairchild."

Ned nodded his head. "That just might do it."

"Ask Sandy to come in on your way down."

Several seconds later, a middle-aged woman with thick glasses entered the office.

"Yes, Chad," she said.

"Get O'Leary on the phone. Tell him number seven is down again and if it's not fixed by the morning, I'll rip out all those damn belts and stop further payments."

Sandy smiled. "You sure you want me to say all that?"

Chad peered at her directly. "What do you think?"

"Okay, okay," she said.

Immediately after she left, the buzzer on the monitor sounded. "Yes," Chad said into the phone receiver. "Yes, put him through."

"Dr. Walker. I'm glad . . ." He stopped talking, obviously interrupted. Almost a minute passed. "Yes, I know that. But

131

it's been almost a week and there's no change. You know if I wasn't going on your enthusiasm, I'd say Margaret is even more uncomfortable." He nodded his head several times, then squinted. "Just a minute, now. You didn't mention it could knock the red blood cell count way down." Chad listened again. He tapped his fingertips on the desk. "Yes, sir, I understand. We give her every support possible. Sure. Okay. We'll give it another week. Thanks for returning my call. Fine. Bye."

He slammed the receiver down and stared at the portrait of his wife at the edge of the desk. A small photo of Sam and Lisa stood beside it. Everything has to have a solution, Chad told himself. He would have traded anything to find a way for Margaret. Medicine seemed so imprecise, so haphazard. If he conducted his business in the same manner, he'd be bankrupt, he assured himself.

Sandy returned to the office. "They can't do it tonight. Their crews are already out."

"Is O'Leary still on?" Chad barked.

"Line 3."

He whipped the receiver off the desk unit again. "Jim, Chad here. I got to have it done tonight." A pause. "Listen, I'm sick of listening to everyone's sob stories. This isn't kindergarten. You come through, like we agreed to in our original commitment, or I'll rip every belt out of the plant and dump it at your doorstep in the morning." Another pause. "If you think I'm kidding, try me . . . just try me!" He pressed another button on the console, disconnecting the call. "Sandy, tell Ned and Petie and Arlen if O'Leary's crew isn't here by five, I want those belts removed. All of them!"

Several minutes later, Ned barged into the room with Petie following him. "Chad," he said. "You're kidding, right?"

"I've never been more serious in my life."

"It could cost us two, three days of production," Petie said. "You'd be cutting your own balls off."

"That's the way I want it done," Chad declared. "They push you around now; they push you around forever."

132

"I don't think that's the issue here. Jim's come through for us before," Ned said. "The man's only human."

"The man's full of shit. If you strike a bargain, you come through."

"Okay," Petie said. "Maybe a little heart."

Chad rose from his chair. He squinted his eyes. "Heart, huh? Where does that get you except dead."

Ned and Petie glanced at each other, confused by the comment.

"O'Leary has until five o'clock, gentlemen; then I want them removed." The two men dipped their heads obediently and exited.

Chad flopped back into his seat. He tried to review some additional orders on his desk, but couldn't concentrate. He picked up the telephone again. "Sandy, get me Dr. Walker." A minute later, the buzzer rang. "Hello. I've been thinking about Margaret's medication. Can't we do better? I mean, this feels like a game of trial and error." A pause. "I know this is your specialty. Maybe there's some way to hit it on several fronts simultaneously." Chad sighed. "No, I'm not saying that. I know you've tried." He nodded his head. "Okay, I'll let you do the worrying. Thanks again."

Just as he hung up the phone, Ned returned with a bunch of papers in his hand. "I need the okay on the Markus order."

"We'll do it later," Chad responded.

"But they need a . . ."

"Later!" Chad shouted, knocking over the portrait of his wife as he pointed to the door. Ned tried to catch the frame as it careened off the desk and splintered on the floor. Without further comment, he left the office.

Chad stared at the empty place on his desk where Margaret's portrait had been. His hands started to shake. Slowly, he rose from the chair, knelt on the ground and began picking up the pieces from the floor. The photograph had been damaged by the broken glass. He tried to smooth the ripped portions with his fingers, fitting the torn layers back together in the same fastidious fashion that he would handle the most delicate elec-

133

tronic components. The breach across Margaret's face bothered him the most. He pushed the punctured area from behind the print and pressed the ruptured edges together. The glass presented a more difficult problem. The large sections fit together like puzzle pieces, but other areas had splintered into a mass of tiny slivers. Nevertheless, Chad attempted to reassemble them.

When Sandy passed the office, she noticed her boss kneeling on the floor. She entered slowly and watched. Chad's hands were shaking visibly now; two of his fingers had been cut by the glass.

"Chad," she said softly, "we can have it reframed." She knelt beside him, aware that he had not heard a single word she had uttered. She tapped him gingerly on the shoulder. "Chad. I'll have it reframed tomorrow. Okay?" He looked at her as if she were a stranger.

"But Maggie's photograph is ripped," he replied. "Good God, it's ripped."

"It's only a photograph," she answered nervously, now frightened by his tone of voice.

"Only a photograph," he echoed.

She picked the frame up with all the pieces of glass in place on top of it. "I'll finish up with this. I think you'd better take care of your fingers."

Chad looked down at his hand, surprised at the tiny trickles of blood visible on his thumb and index fingers. A second later, he felt the pain. The walls of his office seemed to close in around him.

"I have an appointment," he said to Sandy, embarrassed by his actions and his impulse to run. "I'll, uh, be back later . . . maybe."

"We'll hold the fort," replied the woman, infusing her voice with false enthusiasm.

Once in the street, Chad breathed deeply, but the quivering in his hands didn't subside. All he needed was a walk, he told himself. And yet, after eighteen blocks, the underlying tension remained with him. A truck backfired. Chad Millen whipped around, ready to lunge at some unknown assailant. Two more blasts ripped from the vehicle's muffler.

"Get down," someone yelled.

Chad looked into the street and scanned the placid faces of the other pedestrians walking along the sidewalk.

"We can't do it," another voice shouted. And then Chad knew those cries lived in his head; cries he didn't want to remember. As he walked, his feet seemed heavier. The sense of exhaustion began to overwhelm him. He had to find a place to sit down. Chad lumbered across the street and entered the Carlton Hotel lobby. Rather than sit on one of the couches or chairs, he located the telephone booths, entered one, closed the glass door, and lifted the receiver off the hook. The buzz of the dial tone hissed in the small enclosure.

"We got to go back, Lieutenant."

"There's only one way," Chad said, mouthing the words he had barked sixteen years ago to those under his command. All the faces came back to him now.

They had moved out of a village called Fon Li in the morning. Despite air support, the Cong had managed to thin their ranks, bringing down both the captain and the division colonel. If Chad could have influenced the situation magically, he would have implanted another captain and another colonel in their places. But, as he surveyed the troops, he realized that he had, by default, become ranking officer. He had no choice. Almost automatically, he began screaming orders, gathering the men behind a low ridge. Chad knew they couldn't go back; the only possible movement would be forward. They would have to charge through a small glen before they could have the cover of the forest and even that might be infested with the enemy.

"Move it out!" he shouted, using hand signals to reinforce his words. About twenty men leaped over the ridge and raced toward the line of trees. Mortar fire and the ping of bullets striking rocks all around them danced in their ears. Chad gaped at the other sixty men who had not obeyed his order. "Move it! Emery. Laden. Jones. McCarthy. All of you, get going. Let's hit it." Several men got up and began to run first; within seconds, most of the others followed. Chad joined the last wave and darted a jagged course through the field. Most of his men had reached the forest, when machine gun fire spit through the ranks of those still running. Everyone hit the ground. Several men moaned. A few didn't move.

"On your bellies," Chad screamed. "Keep moving. Don't stop. On your bellies." The men began to crawl, leaving their dead behind, but dragging their wounded with them. As Chad snaked his way through the grass, he passed a soldier who lay frozen on the ground.

"Are you hit?" he asked.

The young man didn't answer; he just stared at him.

"Are you hit, soldier?" Chad shouted.

The boy shook his head. His face was smooth, unmarked by even the growth of whiskers.

"Move it out! Now!"

"I can't," the soldier responded.

"Why not?"

"I'm scared," he answered. Tears began to fill his eyes.

Chad became disoriented for a moment. The contact was so personal, so intimate. "Listen, there's no time for that. You have to be strong. Just suck it in. You can do it. Now, c'mon."

"I can't," the boy said. "I'll never make it. We got to go back, Lieutenant."

"There's only one way. There is no 'back.'" Chad looked up and realized that his men had completely cleared the field by now. "You gotta move, otherwise those gunners will get a fix on us."

The young soldier started to cry. "You can't cry, damn it. You've got to be strong. C'mon, I'll help you." As he reached out, the boy panicked, stood up, turned around and charged back toward the ridge. "On your belly!" Chad screamed frantically. The chatter of the machine guns began immediately. A series of bullets stitched a bloody path just above the waist of the running figure, almost cutting his torso in half. He never uttered a sound as he fell to the ground. Chad crawled over to his limp body. The boy's tear-filled eyes stared up at him life-

136

lessly. He grabbed the soldier's shirt angrily and started screaming. "On your belly, I told you. On your belly."

The knocking against the telephone booth door made him aware of the hotel lobby again. A bellhop peered at him. "Are you okay, mister?"

Chad put his finger up and forced a smile. Sweat lathered his hands and face. He placed the receiver back on the hook and opened the door. "Heart," he muttered to himself, "where does that get you except dead?" As he crossed through the lobby, Chad "sucked it in." In ten minutes he would be back in his office. His hands would be steady again. He would smile politely at those around him, knowing that however tentative his apparent victory, he had, at least momentarily, regained control.

The incessant drone of the television filtered through the house like stale smoke, infectious and anonymous. Shafts of sunlight bathed the furniture in the living room and danced off Margaret's collection of watercolors as well as the antique picture frames housing tapestries of another era. The dining room set, a modest reproduction of a museum piece, appeared so neat that the chairs seemed as if they might have been unoccupied for many years. A wooden cane leaned against the wall in the entrance foyer, noticeably clean and spartan without any casual artifacts of everyday living.

In contrast, the kitchen, cluttered with empty plates, soiled napkins, and silverware, seemed the victim of a recent cyclone. Three bags of garbage stood in front of the cabinet under the sink.

Sam threw his books on the kitchen table, narrowly missing the two bowls which represented breakfast for both him and his father. He had awakened late that morning and, therefore, did not do his chores before leaving for school. No regrets. Sam closed his eyes and waved his hand over the dirty dishes in a fashion similar to his friend, Brian, who not only did hand puppet routines, but magic shows as well. Dishes, disappear! he thought to himself. He peeked through a half-opened eyelid; they were still there. Sam smiled at his own game, poured a glass of milk, then searched the bread box for rolls or dough-nuts, a scavenger willing to accept whatever he could find. Only stale bread greeted his probing fingers. He muttered when he opened the refrigerator. Suddenly, he groaned, pausing in the midst of his hunt. He quickly slammed the door, walked back into the entrance hall, and scooted up the stairs three at a time.

Propped up with pillows against the headboard, Margaret Millen slept uncomfortably in a sitting position. Her face, paler and bonier than before, seemed oddly strained. Wisps of brown hair fell stiffly like straw against her cheeks. Her lips were parched and cracked. A subtle darkness had begun to encircle her eyes.

In one hand, she held the remote control unit for the barking television set, which continued to perform in spite of the lack of audience. In the other hand she gripped an empty coffee cup, her thin fingers wrapped tightly around the handle. On the floor beside her, a stainless steel bedpan, filled to the brim, grew like a mechanical mushroom out of the patterned design of the rug. Piles of books, magazines, and newspapers decorated the top of the bureau. A portable hospital tray, complete with casters, hung over the bed. A half-eaten meal lay wasted on its shiny Formica surface. A thick odor embraced the room like an invisible wreath.

Margaret winced as she coughed, her hands automatically holding her chest. She never opened her eyes, just let herself slip back into the comfort of sleep. Sam watched from the door-way. He tried to remember his mother before the sickness ravaged her body. The smooth skin and bright eyes were gone. Her new face, as he called it, dominated his vision of her. The trips to the beach, Sunday breakfasts in the kitchen, Lisa's art shows, and barbecues on the back lawn had become mere foot-notes of a distant memory; a faded photograph he could not restore.

As he stood at the foot of the bed, he surveyed the tense face contorted in sleep.

139

"Mom," he whispered. No response. "Mom, it's me, Sammy. I'm here."

Lifting her eyelids like lead weights, Margaret managed a slight smile. "Oh, Sammy, how come you're here?"

"It's Wednesday, Ma, my day," he said.

"Why did I think it was Thursday? Guess when you live in one room, one day isn't much different than the next. Come, sit down, tell me about school."

The ritual always bored him, yet he proceeded to describe his day. "Homeroom is homeroom," he chanted. "In math, Starky gave us a surprise quiz on four theorems." He described his world history lessons with inflated enthusiasm, then detailed a chemistry experiment in depth. "And that's it—oh, Leman finished up physics with a twenty-minute dissertation on fusion." Margaret, occasionally letting her eyes close for short periods of time, seemed more relaxed than before. Her son's voice comforted her, bringing activity and life into her shrinking world.

"If I had to learn what you kids learn, I could never make it today," she observed.

"Ah, it's not that hard, Mom," he said. "Do you want something to eat?"

"No, I'm not hungry—must be those new pills Dr. Walker gave me. Been nauseous all morning." She struggled with her next request.

Sam, correctly anticipating her words, interrupted her. "I'm going to empty the pan. Be back in a second." He lifted the metal container, balancing it carefully in his arms. Breathing only through his mouth, he avoided looking directly into the murky liquid. After he poured the contents into the toilet, he used the bathtub spout to run water into the pan. The room began to spin. Sam sat on the rim of the tub, bent down over his knees and placed his head between his legs until the dizziness passed. Once the water ran clear in the pan, he returned to the bedroom.

His mother became absorbed in a soap opera, although her eyes wavered half-open. "Sammy, sit with me for a while."

"In a minute, Ma. Let me take this stuff downstairs," he said, indicating the half-empty yogurt container and bowl of tuna salad. After dumping the leftover food into a bulging garbage bag in the kitchen, he sat down at the table. He held his head in his hands, trying to overcome the nausea. For the past two weeks, three afternoons a week started the same way . . . with the bedpan, then the stomach pains. He ignored the glass of milk on the counter, rocking back and forth on the chair like an infant soothing himself with the rhythm of his own body. Twenty minutes passed before he could bring himself to return.

"Come, sit," his mother motioned. Sammy eased onto the other side of the bed, then focused on the television. More than an hour passed without either of them speaking.

Sam broke the silence. "Do you want something to drink?"

"No. I'm okay. If there's anything you want to do, don't mind me, I'll be all right."

"Well," he said, "maybe I could do some homework, but the TV wigs me out."

She flicked the remote control switch with her thumb, extinguishing both sound and picture.

"*Voilà!*" she declared triumphantly.

Parking himself on the floor, Sam started his math assignment. He chewed on a pencil as he worked. Margaret leafed through a mystery novel until she located a folded page. She cleared her throat several times as if she intended to speak, but then lowered her head to begin reading. They both became absorbed in their separate involvements. Another hour passed.

Margaret muffled a cough, throwing a quick smile to her son. She tried unsuccessfully to suppress a second cough, then a third. Wide-eyed, she held her ribs as her body convulsed, overcome by the hacking spasms. Sam ran into the bathroom, then sprinted back into the room, spilling half the water out of the glass. She sipped some, but her coughing continued. Frightened, Sam pressed his hands against her ribs, fearing that her bones, which had become so brittle, might crack. They both pushed desperately against her chest cavity. His mother managed another weak smile, coughed several more times, then collapsed against the pillows. Perspiration dripped from her forehead. The muscles on the right side of her face twitched. Sam used a towel to dry her skin. He tried to steady his hand as he offered her more water.

"I'll be okay," she assured him, pushing away. "It's probably a reaction to the new medicine. Now don't look so concerned, Sammy, I'm fine."

He pushed out a smile, swallowing his own vomit several times. "I'm not so concerned," he said. "You're going to be fine. Maybe next month, you'll be out of bed. Dad said so." His mother turned away, focusing her attention out the window. She couldn't face his commentary. "Anyway," he continued, "I'm not the greatest nurse."

"You do fine," she said authoritatively. Margaret turned back to her son. "You're quite a kid, Sammy." Her eyes filled with tears.

He stared into her face, tongue-tied, wanting to scream, choking on the knot growing in his stomach. "Well," Sam suggested in a purposely sedated voice, "want to watch more of the boob-tube?" When she nodded, he picked up the remote unit and tuned in a game show. Too upset to return to his homework, he watched the program with her, barely absorbing the electronic pantomime.

Another hour passed until Chad Millen arrived home, carrying Chinese food in a brown paper bag. The aging and sadness evident around his eyes diminished the impact of his easy agility and once youthful smile. Only strangers noticed the permanent grimace etched on his face.

"Well, well, two of my favorite people in one room," he declared, tapping Sam on the shoulder and then kissing Margaret affectionately. "How did it go today, honey?"

"Fine," Margaret smiled. "Just fine. You know, Sammy's doing wonderful things in chemistry. Right, Sammy?" He nodded his affirmation.

"You guys mind if I go downstairs now?" Sam asked his parents.

"Hey, I just got home," Chad said as he removed his tie. "How about a little time together? All of us."

Sam sat down on the edge of the bed. "What do you want to talk about, Dad?"

"Everything. Anything. You see the Jets' game today? Some spectacular quarterbacking." Suddenly he stopped himself. "Hey, Mag, I'm sorry, that's got to be boring for you."

"No, no, please go on," she said, settling back for the inevitable—an immense commentary on football, followed by some quips about his office, oscilloscopes, and the inequity of taxes.

"Well, okay," Chad began. "According to the paper, in the third quarter—and they were behind three goals . . . three goals, imagine that."

Sam watched his father's lips, but never heard a word.

17 ᔕᔑ ᔕᔑ ᔕᔑ ᔕᔑ ᔕᔑ ᔕᔑ ᔕᔑ ᔕᔑ ᔕᔑ ᔕᔑ ᔕᔑ ᔕᔑ ᔕᔑ ᔕᔑ ᔕᔑ ᔕᔑ ᔕᔑ

As the sun disappeared behind a distant ridge, splashes of orange and red streaked the horizon. The fading daylight entrapped the green fields in a misty purple; the foliage blended into a darkened landscape. The stillness of the trees on this windless night accented the slapping of our sneakers against the surface of the cinder track. Sam and I had run seven laps together. At his request, we maintained a kind of ceremonial silence. The flapping of wings above us drew our attention. A black bird, perhaps a crow, hovered in the darkness, then lifted skyward and vanished behind the trees. Sam looked at me, quizzically, as if he had a question, but then peered back at the track.

"Ready when you are," I said softly, suddenly aware of being a touch winded.

"The pains in my stomach are getting worse, Bears. Especially on certain days."

"Which days are those, Sammy?"

He angled his head to the side and peered at me. "I know you know. The days I help out with my mother. Sometimes, the pain really takes over. Even had them at track. It's scary."

"What's scary about them?" I asked.

Sam picked up his speed slightly as we began the last lap. "I know it'll sound crazy, being I'm still young and all, but I don't want to get sick or anything. A kid in my class had an ulcer. He's a wreck. Boy, that's all I need now."

"Do you think your stomach pains mean you're getting sick?"

Sam shook his head affirmatively. "Yes. I don't care what the doctor said. Last week I told my grandfather. I didn't want to worry Dad." He stole a glance at me, then lowered his eyes quickly. "Anyway, Papa Charlie promised he wouldn't tell anyone if I went to the doctor with him. I had to drink this white chalk for the X rays—it was awful. Big deal; the man said I was as healthy as a horse, nothing wrong except I had to learn to relax. He gave me some medicine, but it makes me sleepy. I'm not stupid; they were tranquilizers—I could tell because some of the kids sell the same stuff in the lunchroom. Maybe the pills made the pain better, but they sure don't stop them from happening."

"Okay," I said as we rounded the last quarter mile. "Describe the pains, when do you first notice them, how long do they last?"

"Like I said, they happen mostly when I'm with Mom. Sometimes I just lift the bedpan and I can feel them. They get so bad I think I'm going to choke. Once it starts, it can last all night. I want to be with her; I do," he asserted adamantly. "I want to help, but it's really hard."

"What's hard about it?"

"Have you ever carted what's in a bedpan?" I nodded my head. He seemed surprised. "Then you know!"

"Sammy, my reaction to carting a bedpan is mine, yours is yours. Although we might have done the exact same activity, our feelings about it could be very different. What's hard for you in carrying the pan?"

"The stuff, for Christ's sake . . . the stuff in it. I get nauseous every time I look at it, and let me tell you, I never, never look directly into it. I get sick just from the little I catch out of the corner of my eye."

"What's sickening about it?"

"What it looks like. The—the odor."

145

"Sammy, why is that sickening?" I asked as we completed the last revolution.

"It's just sickening," he answered. "Maybe I'm just allergic to it or something. Every time I pick it up, I feel that way."

"What's your first thought when you pick it up?"

"Oh God, that it's hers. My own mother's! Not some stranger's, but my mom's." He shook his head several times. "I think if it was someone else's, then, maybe, it'd be different. But it's not somebody else's."

"What about it being your mom's do you find so . . . uncomfortable?"

"I know what it means, Bears, I really do," he shouted.

"Okay," I said softly, ". . . what do you believe it means?"

He began to sweat profusely. "She's . . . she's . . ." Sam aborted the sentence, squinting his eyes angrily.

"She's what, Sammy?"

"I can't say it. I can't think it." He pressed his hands against the side of his head and ran even faster. I increased my pace to maintain a position alongside of him. "At first," he whispered, "I thought I couldn't because nobody in the house ever talked about it. But it's different. I can't say it."

"Why not?"

"Maybe it'll happen if I do," he said.

"Are you saying that if you say something, that will cause it to happen?"

"Sounds crazy, doesn't it? Somehow, if you say it, it'll be real and I don't want it to be real. Yet I can't stop thinking it. I can't!"

"Why do you believe saying it will make it come true?"

"I don't know, Bears. I don't know why I believe it. Maybe it's like thinking a bad thought."

"What do you mean?"

"Look what happens every time I pick up the bedpan. I feel nauseous, dizzy, like I'm going to puke."

"Are you saying the thought makes you that way?" I asked.

146

"Not exactly," he replied. "When I think it, that's the way I feel."

"Why is that?"

" 'Cause I don't want it to happen. Sometimes I can talk about her not being here, but not the other way."

"What other way?"

"Using the word," he said. "How come words are so powerful?"

"They're not," I answered. "They only have the power we give them. One man screams something vulgar and another person gets upset. Another man screams the same thing and nobody cares. It depends, Sammy. It depends on what we believe about the words."

"Well," he said, "in my house, certain words are very important. They're the ones nobody uses. It's like that word . . . cancer." His eyes twitched nervously. "That's what Mom had all the time, ya know—only everyone said it was anemia. I guess I kind of knew—that's why I went to the library. My father never used that word or the other. Never!"

"Do you want to share what that other word is?"

"Not yet. I'm not ready yet. Could we stop talking now?"

"Why?"

"Let's just finish. I'll meet you on the bleachers." He lunged forward, increasing his speed significantly for the last two laps. I followed his lead, pushing myself until I came alongside of him. Sam held his mouth strangely ajar; his eyes bulged. His strained appearance had little to do with his running.

When I became winded, I concentrated on one distant point . . . the marker at the far end of the track. Sam broke through the imaginary barrier first, completing his tenth mile. I finished my third, easing into a trot, then finally a walk. We paced each other around for another quarter-mile. Sam kept a substantial distance between us.

I sat half-Lotus style on the top bench of the bleachers. Sam dangled his body over three levels. A silver light bathed his face.

"I'm . . . I, it," he stuttered, squeezing out the words with extreme difficulty. "When I . . . lift the, the pan, I know! I know! I know!" He began to shout. His fingers dug into his face. "I know. Nobody will tell me, but I know! She's . . . she's . . . she's going to . . . *die*." Sam screamed the last word. He stood up, snapping his body off the wood plank, and gaped at me—surprised, confused, relieved. For a long time, he held his breath, his body remaining rigid, frozen at attention like a young soldier. A sudden gust of wind rippled through his hair, moving his curls like grain in a farmer's field. Suddenly, he groaned and dropped down on the bench.

I moved closer to him. "Sammy, I'm here. I'm still with you. How do you feel?"

"Weak. Like I have a fever." He stared down at the track and said, "Die. Die. Die. Oh, God, I was so scared to say it. Thought it a thousand times, but couldn't say it. And now, look. Die. Die." He smiled queerly. "It's not so bad. Why did I think it would be so bad? When I was eight, I had a parakeet. His name was Chipper. Boy, I loved that dumb bird, always getting out of the cage and flying all over the house. One day when I came home from school, he wasn't there. They said he flew away, out the door. Well, I looked for him for days and days. I kept calling him in the backyard. Maybe Chipper was cold or hungry. I cried myself to sleep every night for weeks. Then, Lisa, I guess she couldn't stand listening to me any more, came into my room and told me. She said my parents lied, that Chipper had died and there was no use in looking for him any more. No use at all. I hated my parents for that, for all the times I looked for nothing. Then I thought, if they couldn't tell me, dying must be terrible. Everything changed. Chipper wasn't coming back. Dying meant not coming back, no hope to make it change."

"How does the word apply in your mom's case?"

"It's like making it real by saying it could happen. I guess I don't want it to be real." Tears flooded his eyes. "But it is, Bears, I know it is. In my history book, pictures of all the great men have dates under them. When they were born; when they died. It's so matter-of-fact in class . . . *being you or someone you know.*" A . . . up hope. And I don't want to."

"Then why would you?" I asked.

He ignored my question. His eyes filled with . . . der if she knows?"

"Who?"

"My mother. Sometimes, I see her looking funny at he . . . ce in the mirror. I wonder what she's thinking. But she's doing it, too, Bears. Nobody talks about it. I wish . . . I wish we would. It's much more scary when we don't." Sam Millen began to cry. As he leaned his head against my shoulder, I put my arms around him. A few minutes passed before his sobbing subsided and he spoke again.

"Why can't dying be happy? Why does it have to be so sad?"

"Why does it make you sad?" I asked in a voice just above a whisper.

"Because I'll miss her, I really will. Remember what I said . . . about our special relationship. That was a lie, it really was. She's always nice to me, but we don't talk. There's so many things I can't tell her . . . or him."

"Why not?"

"It's that same stuff again. In my house, you don't talk about everything, just some things."

"What are you afraid would happen if you talked about the things you wanted to talk about?"

"They'd get mad."

"Since you don't talk about those things, how do you know that?"

He grinned weakly. "Well, maybe they wouldn't—but maybe they would."

"And if they did get mad, then what?" I asked.

"Then nothing," he concluded, shrugging his shoulders. "That's the big joke. They'd get mad, maybe yell, and that would be the worst of it." He shook his head back and forth.

way it felt, you'd think the atomic bomb
. . . . when I opened my mouth.''

. . . nd now?''

"It's all beginning to look different. I've always been afraid
of words, but you don't have to be, you can use them . . . like
now, like right now. I'm sick of the football crap, the TV, the
'what-did-you-do-in-school' questions. Nobody asks me how I
feel. Never. And I guess I learned really well, because I don't
tell them or ask them either.''

"Do you want to change that, Sammy?''

"Yup. I want to talk more, like this . . . with, with everyone.''

"How are you feeling?''

"Better. Everything doesn't seem so dark.''

Although the clutter in the Millen master bedroom had increased visibly over the past few weeks, Chad maintained everything in a certain order. Books and magazines, even get well cards, had designated places on the floor, on top of the bureau and on the night tables. Uncomfortable about usurping his wife's realm directly, he waited until she fell asleep each night before puttering around in the bedroom. Despite the secrecy of his efforts, Margaret could see the fruits of his labor, a fact which made her feel self-conscious and quite useless. She considered protesting, wanting desperately to maintain some role in the family. And, yet, each time she peered into her husband's sad eyes, she couldn't bear to raise the issue. Chad was her hero and now she blamed herself for making him vulnerable. She could endure the isolation, she told herself as she leaned back against the pillows propped up behind her.

Margaret sat in her bed like a faded princess, gazing out the window. Tiny branches and leaves fluttered against the glass panes. A thick bank of clouds enshrouded the treetops. She reached over and pressed a button on the console. A red light popped on, indicating that the motor drive for the window had been engaged. It opened slowly. The sounds of car horns, birds, and children's laughter filled the room. Margaret smiled weakly, touched the button a second time, and watched the window close. Her eyelids began to fall. For a moment, she fought the gnawing fatigue, never quite sure whether she felt more victimized by her illness or by the drugs which she consumed obediently.

"I'm still me," she whispered to the walls as she fell asleep.

Rather than glide into a sedate state of slumber, Margaret began to dream. An eerie glow lightened her darkened room. The window opened again, then closed, then opened and closed again on its own. Two red lights above the activating switch flashed incessantly. The television set came on automatically. The dial turned through one revolution of channels slowly, then escalated in speed, flashing subliminal images on the luminous screen. The set clicked off, then on again and off again, all in the same rhythm as the window opening and closing. Doorbell chimes filled the bedroom. The video monitor on the console flashed a puppet version of Chad at the door, then clicked off. The doorbell rang again. Now the monitor showed puppet versions of Sam and Lisa together at the door. Suddenly, the screen went blank. Margaret watched herself sleeping in the bed. She shouted her own name in an attempt to waken her inert form, but couldn't.

The three, life-sized puppets reappeared suddenly on top of the bureau. Like a synchronized dance group, they leaned forward in unison, their faces fashioned with duplicate plastic smiles. When they spoke, their voices had a metallic, computerized quality.

"How was your day?" the Chad puppet asked.

Suddenly, Eddie's voice pierced the room. "Maggie," he called.

"How was *your* day?" the Sam puppet chimed.

Eddie's voice sounded again. "Maggie, it's Eddie. Please answer me, Maggie. We're supposed to have a card game, remember?"

The three puppets faced Margaret together and began chattering simultaneously. "How was your day, how was your day, how was your day?" they asked over and over again.

"Maggie," Eddie called, trying to make himself heard

above the mechanical voices of the puppets. "Maggie, I'll talk to you. Please, don't leave me."

Margaret opened her mouth to call to him, but no sounds came from her throat.

The puppets laughed.

"But I am here!" she screamed finally, breaking her sleep and bolting upright in her bed. Her chest heaved as she stared at the books on top of the bureau. She reached for the phone and began dialing Chad's number, then stopped on the sixth digit. After returning the receiver to the hook, she rolled to the side of the bed and grabbed the eight-by-ten framed photograph of her family. Margaret Millen stared at the group portrait. Her hands began to shake when she realized that the only face in the picture which seemed unfamiliar to her was her own.

19

۶ ۶ ۶ ۶ ۶ ۶ ۶ ۶ ۶ ۶ ۶ ۶ ۶ ۶ ۶ ۶ ۶ ۶ ۶

Chad Millen cleared the table, rinsed the dishes before placing them into the dishwasher, then wiped the counter with fast, efficient movements. No hesitations. No wasted energy. He took special pride in his ability to meet any challenge, any difficulty. In his business, he endured a roller coaster economy, managing to earn a substantial income despite the dramatic fluctuations in the electronics market. If he could accomplish that feat, he believed he could do anything. Although he never viewed himself as a winner, he took refuge in the fact he always found a way to survive . . . on his belly or on his feet.

Initially, his wife's illness threatened to disturb the balance, placing a foreign, unwelcome pressure on him. Yet, despite the erosion of his confidence and the increased demands on his time, he met every obligation, he assured himself . . . breadwinner, father, surrogate mother, part-time cook, and house cleaner. Again, he proved he could survive. When the doctor suggested a full-time nurse, he wouldn't hear of it, volunteering himself and his children to care for his wife. There was never a question of money . . . only, perhaps, a question of style. He considered his alternative highly successful not only in rendering the needed services to his wife, but also in bringing the family closer together. Not once did Chad ever doubt his own conclusion, nor did he ever substantiate them by soliciting the feelings of his children.

The ceiling in the kitchen acted like a baffle for the television set which blared from the master bedroom above. The crackling of gunfire, explosions, and screams filled the room. Chad found the noise soothing, a predictable lullaby, a mindless antidepressant. "Thank God for that set," he thought to himself, paying silent tribute to the electronic companion which he believed had diverted Margaret from thinking about her situation. The buzzer on the coffee machine drew his attention. He pushed a blue button, then poured himself a cup of the black liquid. Settling down by the table, he immersed himself in the *Wall Street Journal*. Though he had read the paper once on the train, he took comfort in a second reading, occasionally testing his memory and surprising himself with his ability to retain information.

Sam walked into the kitchen silently, his sneakers cushioning his footsteps. His father looked up, startled. "Hey, how about a little noise or something? You could scare someone half to death that way."

One word lunged out of the sentence—the very word which had dominated Sam's thoughts since his last session. Death. Dying. The taboo subject, one among many. Ironically his father had used it, though in an impersonal context. "I'll be sure to wear my boots next time," Sam said.

"No sarcastic remarks now. Sit down, I'll be finished in a minute." Chad scanned the last several pages quickly. The self-satisfied smile on his face seemed stiff and oddly familiar to his son, like an old mask, overused and unconvincing. Rubbing his hands together briskly, he said, "So, how'd it go at school today?"

"You really want to know?"

"Yes, I really want to know!" his father insisted, slightly offended by his son's question.

"Well, in Social Science II, we watched film strips on inventors and their early inventions like the cotton gin, the telephone, the steam engine. In math, we learned two more theorems in solid geometry. In English, my teacher bored us to death with a lecture on *A Portrait of the Artist As a Young Man* by James Joyce. Boy, he writes a lot better than my teacher talks. In gym . . . let me see, oh yes, in gym we did the same old calisthenics, the same old running and jumping exercises. What else? Wait, wait, I know there's something else.'' Itemizing his courses with his fingers and his words, he said, ''Social science, math, English, gym . . . ah, yes, yes, I have it. How could I forget? Dear Dr. Jacobs, my chem instructor, started a fire in the lab. That was the most exciting part of the day.'' He noticed his father stealing glances at the paper while he talked. ''Dad?''

''Uh-huh?''

''What book did we discuss in my English class?''

''Whatever you said.''

''I know what I said; I just wanted to see if you were listening.''

''Sammy, I was listening and I refuse to be tested,'' Chad said, his face flushed. ''I don't know what's getting into you lately. I thought those sessions with Grandpa's friend would calm you down.''

''I don't need to be calmed down,'' Sam said softly. ''I'm not the one who's angry!''

Chad eyed his son suspiciously. ''I'm not changing my mind; we all decided, especially your take-charge grandfather, that it would be good for you to talk to Mr. Kaufman. But what do you get out of those conversations anyway?''

''Plenty,'' he replied. ''They really help.''

''Good, that's good,'' Chad said. He forced a smile, unwilling to probe further, then allowed the paper to attract his attention once again.

''Dad, can we talk?''

Detecting a change in his son's voice, Chad, camouflaging his annoyance, folded his hands on the table and said, ''Sure. We always talk. You don't need to make an announcement.''

''Maybe I do,'' Sam said. ''Maybe I do because I don't

mean the kind of talk we just began. I'm talking about saying things straight to each other.''

"I still don't understand what you're talking about," his father retorted. "I always talk straight to you. That's the way everyone is in this house. What are you getting at?"

"What about Ma?"

"What about her?" Chad barked.

"Please," Sam said. "I don't want you to be angry."

Chad exhaled a deep breath, then said, "I'm not angry. Just a little short these days. I don't mean to jump on you. What about your mother?"

"How is she?" Sam asked, his voice almost a whisper.

"Well, Dr. Walker changed the medicine again. The results are promising. Nothing for you to worry about. She'll probably be up and around in a month. By that time, you won't remember she was ever sick.''

"But, Dad, that's what you said two months ago, then two months before that.''

"What is this . . . an inquisition? Forget what I said two months ago, or at any other time. Listen to what I say now. She'll be fine.''

"How can you be sure? Did the doctor say she would be fine in a month?"

Folding the paper carefully, Chad fumed. "I don't think I like you talking this way to me, do you hear?" Sam nodded his head. "Furthermore, we're all under a great strain. Let's not quarrel.''

"Do you want some juice?" Sam asked, retreating from the table.

"No. I'm still not finished with this cup of coffee.''

Edging back toward his father, Sam spoke quietly. "I really don't want to fight. I'd like to talk. Can't we talk?"

"Well, I think we talked enough for tonight." Chad looked down at the folded paper and started to read the two exposed columns.

"Is Ma going to die?"

"Where the hell did you get that idea? She's doing fine. You hear! That's it, that's it, she's doing fine." He shook his head, avoiding his son's eyes. "I don't want any more of that kind of talk. No more."

"But I think about it, Dad, all the time. If I think about it, why can't I talk about it?"

"That's not the question. The question is whether you're going to listen to me or not. If I say the discussion is over, it's over. Finished! Now I don't have to keep going on with you. It's late, go to bed."

Sam left the kitchen, only to return several minutes later. "Dad?"

"You're really pushing it tonight, Sammy. I thought I told you to go to bed."

"I care about Mom very much, very much. So I'd like to say something."

"I guess you'll go on forever unless I let you get it off your chest," Chad sighed. "Okay, you care about your mother. Now what?"

Drawing in a deep breath, Sam's eyelids quivered as he faced his father directly and said, "I think she's going to die . . . soon."

Jumping out of his chair, Chad slapped Sam across the face; the impact threw him against the cabinets. He grabbed his son by the shirt and raised his hand again.

"Go ahead," Sam said coldly. "It won't change what I think, it won't change it." Chad hesitated. His body trembled as he glared at his son. Then he surrendered himself to his anger and brought his hand down against his son for the second time, slamming him to the floor. The boy started crying. His father turned away swiftly and stormed out of the house.

Holding on to the side of the counter, he pulled himself off the floor, dazed, beyond tears. Like a zombie, he began to clear the table, going through the motions, the ritual, mechanically rinsing the coffee cup and juice glass, then placing them neatly into the dishwasher. He couldn't remember the last time his father hit him. His face felt hot and swollen. Sam stopped himself from crying again.

"Dad," he called, inching his way toward the entrance hall. "Dad, are you there?"

The front door was wide open. Nervously, Sam backed into the kitchen. Had his father gone crazy? Without delaying any longer, he ran outside, never looking back, never noticing his mother balanced uncomfortably on her cane as she leaned against the wall at the top of the stairs.

The street was deserted. He searched the darkness, looking for his father in the shadows. "Pop! Pop!" No response. Suddenly, he noticed the figure of a man sitting on a bench in front of the park. He ran down the street, feeling very alone. The sound of his sneakers slapping the pavement bounced off the houses and reverberated in his ears. As he approached the bench, he stopped running, becoming more cautious with each step. Sam recognized the man's shirt. Then he heard it; the unfamiliar and devastating sound of his father sobbing. He had never seen him cry. He thought of running away, but stopped himself. Fighting back his own tears, he drew nearer to the bench, peering at the hunched figure and the hands cupping his head. Sam remembered his session on the bleachers and his victory over the word "death." He was no longer afraid.

Sitting beside his father, he put his hand on the man's shoulder. He didn't speak, just sat there quietly, waiting. After several minutes, the sobbing ended. Chad had spent his emotions.

He rose from the bench unsteadily, turned away from his son, then spoke in a voice barely audible. "I'm sorry, Sammy. If I could cut off my hand, I would. I know I can't take it back. In a way, it had nothing to do with you."

"It's okay, Dad. I got a hard head."

Chad nodded. "Thought I had it under control. I guess I don't. You see, Sammy, I believed if we all just thought good thoughts, remained positive, everything would turn out. But I guess that's like living a lie. I know it sounds childish, but I didn't know what else to do. Christ, you're only seventeen and you knew." He smiled warmly at his son. "I kept kidding myself I was doing it for you and Lisa, but when you said that in the kitchen, I realized I was doing it for myself. I didn't want to

159

hear what you said. I didn't want to think it. I . . . I really don't know what I'd do . . . without her. You know what I mean?'' Tears poured down his face.

Sam wiped his eyes continually as he peered at his father. ''Maybe if we talked, like now. Maybe it'll help. That's what I've been doing in the sessions and it really makes a difference.''

He stared at his son proudly. ''I don't know if I could go through that, the talking. Thinking about her not being here. Maybe we could try.'' Chad took a deep breath and threw out his chest like a sergeant drilling his troops. ''Okay, Sammy, try, try me. Go ahead, right now. Talk. Ask a question.''

''You know what I'm going to ask you, don't you?''

''Just ask, Sammy, just ask.''

''Is Ma going to die soon?''

The muscles in his face quivered as he riveted his eyes to his son's. In a very soft, controlled voice, he said, ''Nobody can know that for sure. We've changed the medicine many times now . . . many times.'' He sighed loudly, forcing himself to continue. ''Her blood count is getting worse and worse . . . and worse. I think it's possible, very possible that it could happen soon.''

Sam wrapped his arms around his father. ''Thanks for telling me, Dad.''

''Thank you, Sammy. You're really quite a kid. Maybe it's time we all stopped running away from it.''

As they walked back to the house, arm in arm, Sam nudged his father. ''What about Ma?''

''What about her?''

''Does she know?''

''No, not really. I don't know what she guesses. I keep telling her it's getting better when it's not. She has to keep her spirits up. That's so, so important.''

''But maybe she thinks about it too . . . like me and you. Maybe she'd want to talk about it.''

Chad clamped his hand down hard on his son's shoulder. ''I know what you're going to say next. Now, forget it. You hear?

160

Don't you dare talk to your mother about her sickness. Don't you dare use that word in front of her! She needs all the strength she can get." He pulled his son close to him, embracing him tightly. "Sammy, listen to me. I'll talk to you about it, any part of it, any time. I won't keep anything from you any more. I promise. Only, your mother stays out of this. Please, Sammy, trust me."

๛๛๛๛๛๛๛๛๛๛๛๛๛๛๛๛๛

20

Three young women dressed in black leotards did a tap dance routine on the sidewalk in front of an antique store. A mime, directly across the street, impersonated a parking meter in order to collect donations from passing pedestrians. An elegantly attired man stood at the corner of Seventh and West 4th, oblivious to those who stopped and gaped at the falcon perched on his shoulder. He made no effort to camouflage his gloved hand or the thick leather pads sewn to the arms on his jacket. Sam joined a group of people and gawked at the bird, then at its master. Their frozen positions made them appear momentarily unreal, but then both man and bird blinked. Several people laughed. Sam smiled. I'm just like a tourist, he thought as he turned and headed toward Bleecker. New York City's Greenwich Village represented a foreign culture to him. Russian wolfhounds, purple hair, and roller-skating jockeys became mere footnotes for the unpredictable assemblage of oddities confronting him. And yet, he enjoyed the exposure, even today, when he ventured into the city for his second visit with Lisa on her home turf. He always pictured his sister in his parents' house, living in the room next to his, despite the fact she had moved out almost three years ago. Her choice of neighborhoods in Manhattan perplexed him. She was no longer predict-

162

able. Do you ever know anyone, really know them? he wondered.

The facade of the converted factory appeared no different from the adjoining building, except for the massive wood door which had been recently oiled and polished. Sam peeked into the window of the flower shop on the main floor before entering the structure. He stood in front of an old elevator for several minutes, hesitant about boarding. Finally, he hopped aboard, pressed the sixth-floor button, and positioned himself against the back wall as the large cubicle groaned its way up the ancient shaft. Could he do it? he questioned. Would she hate him for trying to get through? He knocked on the door to Lisa's loft five times until he generated a response.

"Well hello, Mr. Millen," Jessica said, bowing ceremoniously as she opened the door. "So you honor us with your presence a second time in one year. We are humbled by such generosity."

"Hi, Jessie," he replied warmly.

She looked at him curiously for several seconds. "You look different, Sam."

He smiled awkwardly and entered.

"Sammy!" Lisa called from the studio area. She left her chisel on the butcher block and moved toward her brother with a huge grin. "This clay hardens real quick. Give me ten more minutes on this piece and I'm all yours. Okay?"

Sam nodded as they kissed each other lightly on the cheek. "And," she added, returning to the other section of the loft, "take whatever you want from the refrigerator."

"Except the chocolate mousse," Jessica interjected.

The idea of having many different rooms as one big open area still seemed peculiar to Sam. No privacy. No place to retreat. He grabbed a magazine from the table and flopped down onto the couch. Instead of reading, he watched his sister using her tools like surgical instruments. Her movements reminded him of his mother. Lisa squinted her eyes several times. Her hair, obviously combed in honor of her brother's visit, curled over her shoulders. She seemed pleased. Even Jessica appeared

163

playful scatting some jazz phrases while applying dark stain to long planks of wood destined to be bookshelves.

As Sam studied the art studio area more closely, he became mesmerized by the light engulfing the room. Although it emanated from both the large window and skylight, the most intense stream of light fell directly on Lisa, making her form and the other objects therein appear washed and muted. Suddenly, he spotted what he deciphered as a self-portrait of Lisa, which had that same undefined quality. He brought his hands up to his eyes and curled them, forming binoculars to bring the painting more clearly into focus. That's not Lisa, he concluded; it's Mom. Dropping his hands quickly to his side, he had an impulse to run out. Maybe this wasn't the right move, he thought, vacillating between self-confidence and fear.

The ten minutes Lisa had requested to complete her sculpture expanded into over half an hour. Finally, she sighed noisily and joined her brother on the couch.

"Thanks for being so patient. Now, let's see . . . how's it going at school?" she asked.

He would have confronted her question now and stopped her there, putting an end to the old Millen routine, but Jessica's presence made him somewhat reticent. He decided to wait. In the interim, he answered his sister's questions with the same pantomimed enthusiasm he had displayed with his mother. Fifteen minutes later, the process reversed. Sam asked the questions and Lisa itemized the events unfolding in her life. They skimmed the surface, as they had been taught to do, maintaining the conversation within safe boundaries. Feelings and fears had been conspicuously omitted.

After changing her outfit behind an oriental screen, Jessica flashed a toothy grin in the smoked, ornate mirror. "Ta-ta," she sang to Sam and Lisa. "Hey Sam, maybe next time you'll come with me and I'll show you a New York you've never seen," she joked, winking and rolling her eyes. No one answered. Responding to Lisa's grimace, she added, "He's a big boy darling. It's about time he learned all about the real world." She flitted out the front door.

164

Lisa and Sam sat motionlessly for almost a minute. No one spoke.

Lisa bounced off the couch and headed for the kitchen. As she filled the teapot, she said, "You know, you're awfully quiet for a guy who came here to talk."

"I'm trying, Lise."

She glanced at her brother; his sincerity touched her in a very special way. Lisa saw herself as apart from her family. Sam's softness allowed her to feel closer. She removed two mugs from the cabinet and a box of herbal tea from a nearby shelf. For a couple of minutes, they both took refuge in the silence between them.

Finally, Sam sat upright and clasped his hands on top of his knees. "I—uh—I want to talk to you about Mommy . . . about, uh, about Mom's dying."

Lisa froze for a moment, then continued her domesticity. "Do you want honey in your tea?"

"Didn't you hear me, Lisa? I said, Mom's . . ."

"I heard you!" she screamed, twirling around and glaring at her brother. Her head quivered uncontrollably. "You're doing this to get back at me for Jessie, aren't you?"

"No, no, Lisa," Sam countered. "I'm doing this—to *be* with you." He struggled to organize his thoughts. "I don't know what else to do except tell you what I know and how I feel. Is that wrong?"

The softness apparent in his face disarmed her. She searched for an honest answer. "I don't know if I'm ready to have this conversation."

An awkward pause.

"I know I'm younger, Lisa, but maybe I can help," he said.

"Maybe," she mumbled, echoing his thoughts as she poured the hot water into the cups.

Lisa Millen closed her eyes and massaged an area just below her rib cage while inhaling a deep breath. This is it, she thought, bracing herself against the sink for added support. Her hands pressed against the porcelain surface. Slowly, very slowly, Lisa disengaged and walked to the couch, unable to control the quivering liquid spilling over the tops of the mugs she carried. After placing them on the coffee table, she searched her mind for some other diverting activity. Nothing came. Finally, she flopped into the soft pillows of the couch and allowed her eyes to face Sam's.

"You know, Sammy, ever since Mom got sick, I've had this knot right here that gets so tight sometimes I feel like screaming." She paused. "Okay, Sammy . . ," she conceded, nodding her head, "okay, I'm ready."

Sam knew the feelings. His eyes watered, not from unhappiness, but because, at that moment, the love he felt for Lisa was almost too much.

Somehow, this time, Sam found it easier to talk about his mother and the reality of the situation. Lisa listened to her brother without trying to fight back the tears. She held his hands so tightly that her fingers left tiny bruises on the surface of his skin.

In the silence that followed Sam's soliloquy, Lisa buried her head in Sam's shoulder. He encircled her with his arms. Their bodies joined together rhythmically in an almost imperceptible rocking motion.

"The knot's gone," Lisa acknowledged in a faint whisper.

Sammy tightened his grip and drew his sister closer to him.

Most of the musicians played their parts at the precise moment the conductor cued them. Although the skills of the students varied dramatically, they had managed to develop a genuine camaraderie during the orchestra rehearsals. The turbulence of the Wagnerian overture kept their attention. Ginny stared at her teacher. She had memorized both the melody and countermelodies and waited anxiously for her entry into the movement. Counting seven measures after the kettle drummer began his roll, she drew in a deep breath, held it, tightened her lips, depressed two keys, then committed the entire contents of her lungs to her French horn. The brass section signaled an emotional turning point in the music. They raced toward a crescendo with such intensity that the teacher had to hold his hands up, trying to slow their pacing.

After a few minutes of continuous playing, Ginny released the mouthpiece from her lips and waited for the next part. Her eyes scanned the almost empty auditorium. Only five seats out of five hundred were occupied. Suddenly, she noticed Sam, who appeared to be looking directly at her. He smiled and waved. She acknowledged his greeting by tipping her head. As the French horn section began to play again, Ginny realized she had missed her cue. She jerked her instrument off her lap and stumbled into the overture.

After two hours of rehearsal, the conductor dismissed the class. Ginny, carrying her French horn case, exited slowly through the side door. Once she spotted Sam leaning against the wall, she separated from the other musicians and walked toward him.

"Hi," she said, and then hesitated. "How come you're here?"

"I came to listen to you play."

"Oh." Ginny smiled.

"Great horn section." Sam tugged on his collar. "You doing anything this afternoon?"

"No."

"Good," he said, "I have an idea. I'd like you to meet my mom. You'd like each other."

Ginny was too flustered by his suggestion to answer immediately. Finally, she replied. "Oh! Uh, sure, Sammy. I'd . . . I'd like that too."

He took the French horn from her and carried it as they walked together down a path leading from the school.

"Ginny . . ." Sam began hesitantly, "tell me about your dad."

"Really?"

"Really," he declared.

While Ginny detailed her father's illness and ultimate death, Sam was acutely aware of the love she had and still felt for him, but without the accompanying pain and tears he had always believed went hand in hand. Something warm and calming washed through his system like an internal shower.

By the time they reached his house, Sam had already shared his mother's situation with her, explaining his past disjointed flight from the drugstore, and his own evolution through talks with a friend of his grandfather.

"One day you'll meet him," he said, "his name is Bears." They both laughed.

"Many times I think about all the things I would have said and done differently if I hadn't been so scared—and if everyone else in my family wasn't scared too."

"Yeah! I know," Sam nodded.

They climbed the steps to the door of the house. Ginny stopped in the middle of the staircase.

"It's okay, Ginny. My mom's a doll. You'll see."

Suddenly, the door opened mechanically. They chuckled.

"That's one of the things I told you about that my dad rigged up. C'mon in." He waved at the camera above his head.

"Sammy," Maggie's voice rang out from the speaker beside the door.

"Yup. It's me, Mom, and I have a surprise for you," he called back.

Bolting up the stairs, two at a time, Sam told Ginny, "Be right back. Just want to check on my mom first."

As Ginny watched him disappear into the bedroom, she remembered something her grandmother always told her: "You can always tell how nice a boy is by how he treats his mother."

Was that really always true? she wondered.

Margaret sat up in bed, as usual, and tried to muster up as much excitement in her voice and demeanor as possible.

"Wow! You're a bundle of energy today, Sam. And I see you've brought a friend."

"Yeah," he blushed. "I'd like you to meet her, Mom. Her name's Ginny."

Suddenly, Margaret became terribly self-conscious. "Do I look all right?"

"Sure," Sam said.

168

She ran her fingers through her hair and adjusted the top of her bathrobe. "Well, I guess we can't keep her waiting."

"I guess not," her son replied as he sprinted out of the room.

Margaret couldn't remember the last time Sam brought anyone home . . . and Chad, too, for that matter. But who can blame them, she reasoned.

Ginny, with Sam at her side, entered the room cautiously.

"Well, hi there, Ginny," initiated Margaret. "Isn't this a wonderful surprise!" She smiled broadly at both of them. "Listen, I know it's not often you get to visit with people in their bedrooms, but . . . I just do it for effect."

"Mom!" Sam protested playfully.

"A woman's prerogative," Ginny quipped. "Right, Mrs. Millen?"

Maggie winked.

Ginny relaxed. After about a half hour of conversation, she even allowed herself to play the French horn for Sam's mother. When she finished a Bach suite, both Margaret and Sam applauded. Ginny smiled bashfully.

"What a wonderful gift you've given me today, Ginny. Thank you."

"Sam told me you love *Peer Gynt*. I'm going to learn it and play it for you."

Uncomfortable in the upright position, Margaret leaned back against the headboard. Suddenly, she began to cough. She hunched forward and held her rib cage. Sam glanced at Ginny and then at his mother. Before he could get to her to help her, the hacking spasm subsided.

"You get some rest, Mrs. Millen," Ginny chimed. "I'd like to come back and visit again, if it's okay with you."

Margaret smiled weakly at Ginny and Sam. "I'd like that," she concluded.

A nineteen-foot disk, held vertically, revolved slowly on the surface of one of three ponds set in the shadows of an antiquated monastery. An aluminum spindle soared skyward from its limestone base on top of a knoll. The rusted wings of a sculpted bird stood sentry over a distant meadow.

Sam had agreed to meet me here, at the Fine Arts Center, for his next session. After completing an all-day intensive with another client at this same location, I strolled along the network of paths snaking through this pastoral property, allowing myself a thirty-minute break before his arrival.

As I reached the small Victorian gazebo, the sun peaked through a heavy overcast, gilded the trees in a golden sheath, then disappeared from view. A squadron of green-necked Canadian geese glided along the air currents just beneath the clouds. The muffled horn of a distant train echoed amid unruffled trees. On a nearby grassy slope, I did a series of stretching exercises, then lay down to face the sky. The remaining fifteen minutes passed very quickly.

At five-thirty, the designated time of our appointment, I returned to the gazebo and waited. Five-forty. Five forty-five. No Sam. Suddenly, I heard the fast-paced sound of rubber against macadam. When I saw the lone figure appear over the crest of a hill, I couldn't help but smile. I imagined Sam excited

about being late so that he could legitimatize ru
walking. He moved like a deer—relaxed, gracefu ,
body belonged to the motion, playing out its own inner rhyt .
His legs sliced through the air like long, thin needles, choreo-
graphed for maximum speed.

"Bears," he shouted. "Sorry I'm late." He leaped onto the
bench beside me, more winded than usual. "Everything just
got screwed up at practice."

"It's okay," I said. "You still have any energy left to
walk?"

"Sure."

When we left the shelter of the gazebo, it began to drizzle.
"Ah-ha," I mumbled, staring up at the clouds. "Do you want
to head back?"

"Hey, it's nice," he declared, turning palms up to catch the
thin spray.

"Did you ever run on a beach when it rains?" I asked. Sam
shook his head. "Well," I added, "it's quite a beautiful expe-
rience." When we encountered a wood sculpture which looked
like a beehive, both Sam and I poked our heads inside to dis-
cover a Lucite queen bee staring back at us. I laughed.

"Wow," Sam whispered. "That's neat."

"What would you like to work on?" I asked as we continued
our walk.

"My dad and me, I guess."

"What about it?"

"Sometimes I can't believe it's me. I told him how I felt,
straight out, no bullshit. He rapped me a couple of times, real
hard. I kept thinking he lost his mind. Anyway, we talked. It
was the first time we ever talked like that. He said it . . . she
could die soon, that it was really possible. How come I feel bet-
ter now that I know?"

"What do you think?"

"Maybe I'm just getting used to it," he said. "Not knowing
is worse than knowing. Before I kept making circles in my
head. Now they're gone. Even the stomach pains are gone. Fi-
nally, I can think about other things. I really like our talks. You

. . . you're going to laugh when I tell you, . . . ow okay to think about it and talk about it, I . . . re . . . at least not all the time like I used to."

. . . , it's like the story of a little boy left in a room. Just . . . e kid, listen, do anything you want, play with any- . . . but don't do one thing, don't open the closet. Well, from then on, all the child thinks about is the closet. Sometimes he'll just open it immediately. Sometimes, if he's scared enough, he won't touch the door, but he'll sure play with the idea all the time, worry about it, nurse it, reject it and then reconsider it again. In your house, death is a little like the closet. Everybody knows it's there, but nobody's allowed to open the door because maybe you'll find something terrible. And then if you believe that, you never get to deal with the closet; you're too busy dealing with your fears about the closet."

"And when you finally get to it, it's not the same," he said. "I even had a wonderful afternoon with Ginny. She came back and played for Mom on her French horn." Sam's eyes glowed. "So maybe I'll work more of it out, like I'm doing right now. But with my father, it's different. I'm glad I talked to him, but I still feel bad about what I did to him."

"And what was that?" I asked.

"That I hurt him by what I said."

"What do you mean, Sammy?"

"I told him that I thought she was going to die and he just went crazy. He got so angry and upset. But if I hadn't said that, nothing would have happened."

"Maybe that's true. You said something and then your father responded. But how did you hurt him?"

"I just told you," Sam insisted, "by saying what I did."

"How do your words hurt him?"

"Well, the words don't hurt him. It's what he thinks about the words; you know, I had the same problem before."

"Let's explore it again . . . what you experienced. When someone talked about death and people dying, did you get upset?"

172

"Sometimes. Not in my history class, when it's about someone I never knew, but when I thought about my mother."

"Okay, then sometimes you heard about death and didn't get upset; at other times, you did. Is that so?"

"Yes."

"When you did get upset, did the person who said the word get you upset; was he or she responsible for your feeling sad or unhappy?"

"No, because what they said didn't always matter," Sam replied. "I guess it depended on what I was thinking about."

"So who gets you upset . . . who does it to you?"

He smiled hesitantly. "Well, if it's not them, and it's not, then it must be me. I do it to me. Wow, that's really neat, Bears. I see what you mean."

"It would be nice for you to see that's what 'you' mean. Your 'wow' is not over my question, but your answer, your own realization." He meditated on my comment, then nodded enthusiastically. "Okay," I continued, "back to your father. Do you believe you hurt him?"

"No," he answered. "I guess not. But there's a catch—suppose I know he gets himself upset when I talk about certain things and then I talk about them . . . isn't that kind of doing it to him?"

"What do you think?"

"My answer is no and yes. He'd still do it to himself, but I pressed the button."

"Sammy, you have curly brown hair. If someone told you they hated curly brown hair and they got unhappy every time you walked into the room with your curly brown hair, did you press their button?"

"That would be ridiculous," he mused. "Then anyone could make up a reason to get upset and blame it on you. I think they would have the problem. It'd be the same for me. It's like my friend Jane—she gets upset when anyone mentions she's tall, then screams at them for getting her upset. You gotta see her. She drives herself crazy." Sam paused, allowing a half-grin to surface. "I can see this all now."

"Back to your dad. Did you hurt him?"

"No, but I want to go through it . . . okay?"

"Sure."

"I talked about my mother dying. To my father that's like curly brown hair and he freaks. He does that because he has . . . his reasons, but he doesn't have to get unhappy. So I don't do it to him. That's really clear. I wish I knew this before; it would have been easier to talk to him. Maybe I could have made him understand instead of feeling so guilty . . . like I did something terrible."

Sam picked up a flat stone and skimmed it along the surface of the pond we had just circled. "You know what, I'm glad I did it, for me and for him—I think it was good he talked. You know? And things have been different since then. He's been friendlier the last two days . . . I mean, he smiles at me more. He also told me they're going to try a new kind of chemo . . . um . . . chemotherapy next week. He kept his word."

"How do you feel, Sammy?"

"Like I have a father. Really good. I even talked to Lisa and Ginny; but . . . I'm uncomfortable about how I am with Mom. I'm still a phony. We still do the smiles all the time, like everything was the same. And, maybe, she knows."

Just as he completed the last sentence, it began to rain heavily. We laughed at each other. Soaked during the first seconds of the downpour, I said, "I don't know whether it matters now, but we could either walk or run to the parking lot."

"Then what?"

"My Jeep's there. We'll go back to the house on the hill and continue."

"Okay," Sam said.

We left the path and ran across the meadow.

After showering at the house, I threw our clothes into a dryer. Sam looked comical outfitted in one of my old sweatsuits. We sprinted up the hill, leaped onto the deck, and ran into the one-room studio. Rain pelted the roof and windows.

Once we were seated, Sam said, "Where was I?"

"Do you remember?" I asked.

174

"Yeah, I think so. About my mother, my feeling uncomfortable when I'm with her."

"What is it about being with your mother that makes you uncomfortable?"

"The lie."

"What lie, Sammy?"

"Smiling all the time, saying everything's getting better when it's getting worse, making believe I'm interested in all the things we talk about when I'm not. Feeling one way and acting another way."

"What about doing those things disturbs you?" I asked.

"I want to tell her about how I feel. Maybe she would want to tell me how she feels."

"That might be what you want to do, but that's different than getting unhappy about not doing it. Why does it make you unhappy when you realize you're not sharing your real feelings?"

"Because if it happens, then we never talked, never had that special thing."

"What do you mean?" I asked.

"She could . . . die, and we would never have been together, not really."

"If that came to pass—what you fear—why would you be unhappy?"

"I just would."

"But why, Sammy?"

He stood up and paced the room. "Because at least one time, I'd like to be me. That's the special thing."

"What are you afraid would happen if you weren't unhappy about not having a special thing?"

"Then I wouldn't have it," he asserted, dropping back onto the couch.

"Ah, are you saying by being unhappy, it'll happen easier or be more possible?"

"Yes," he said. "If I weren't unhappy about it, then it wouldn't matter. I'd just let it slide."

"Why do you believe that?" I asked.

"I don't know. I'm getting confused again, Bears. Wouldn't I just forget about it if I wasn't unhappy?"

"Sammy, that might be a nice question for you to answer," I suggested.

He stared at the floor and rubbed his hands together. "Okay," he said, "I wouldn't have to forget about it. I could still want it, I guess."

"Do you have some doubts?"

He shrugged his shoulders.

"Sammy, do you think you have to be unhappy in order to remember you want that special thing, as you call it?"

"No. I don't have to be unhappy to remember. That feels right! It's different from what I thought before, but it feels right." He shook his head, courting a slight smile. "First I think one thing, then when I look at it, I really don't believe it at all. It's all so weird," he concluded, "but I like it."

"What do you want, Sammy?"

"To talk to her," he asserted a second time, his voice dramatically stronger. "What do you think I should do?"

"There's no should, except the ones we decide to put there," I said. "It's that same point we've talked about before. If I give you my opinion, it would tell you what I would do, which, in a real way, has little to do with you. It's your decision. And nobody knows more about you than you do. Not me, not anybody."

"Yeah, but I'm only a kid," he said sarcastically.

"What does that mean?"

"You know, kids don't really know the answers; they haven't lived long enough."

"Do you believe that?"

"Isn't that the line? I hear it in my house, in school, everywhere. 'You're too young, kid, what do you know?' "

"But do you believe it?"

"Sometimes," he answered.

"And now?"

"A little bit."

"Why do you believe it?"

176

"Maybe I don't know, maybe all I'll do is make the wrong decision."

"What do you mean by the wrong decision?"

"It's not only me. It's my mother and my father. Suppose she doesn't want to talk about it like me. That would be awful."

"Why, Sammy?"

"Because then I would have . . ." He threw his head back, stared at the ceiling, and held his breath.

"Why did you stop?" I questioned.

"I was going to say I would have hurt her. But as I thought of the words, I knew they weren't true. I just don't want to see her get any more unhappy."

"Do you believe that's what will happen if you talk to her?"

"Bears, I really don't," he said. "If I was sick, really sick, I'd want someone to talk to me . . . just like she did once. I used to have asthma, a real bad case. I remember being in the hospital, all by myself. It seemed forever. God, I was so scared. Then my mother came and sat with me all day one day and just explained what was wrong; how my lungs were filled with stuff and how the doctors were giving me special medicine to stop the infection so I could breathe better. I think I loved her on that day more than any other day. I wasn't scared after we talked. Maybe I could do that for her, but, somewhere, I'm still afraid."

"Of what?"

"I don't know any more. Could I just be afraid without a reason?"

"What do you think?" I asked.

"That's what it feels like."

"Well, if you don't have a reason to be afraid, why would you be?"

"I guess I wouldn't, Bears. It's going, this fear thing, but I still feel something, just a tiny bit," he acknowledged.

"Sammy, what are you afraid would happen if you weren't afraid?"

He laughed. "You know the answer as well as I do. Then, I'd do it."

"Are you saying you're afraid in order to stop yourself from doing it?"

"Yes. That's kind of dumb—scaring myself. I do it all the time, don't I? Well, I don't feel scared now. I feel freer . . . to decide. And you know what, I want that special thing even more now. Ma would understand, I know she would. But, damn, I wish I never talked to my father."

"Why, Sammy?"

"Because he asked me not to talk to her and he's been great. He wouldn't understand. He'd think I didn't care about anything he said. But I do, Bears, I do."

"You know you do and I know you do, but suppose, as you said, he doesn't know it—how would you feel?"

"Pretty shitty," he snapped.

"Why?"

"It's like he trusted me, told me everything, and then I did this. I guess I think he'd never trust me again."

"And what about that would make you unhappy?"

"I'd be alone, all over again."

"What's disturbing about being alone?"

"No one to talk to," he said. "Round and round in circles."

"Why would that make you unhappy?"

"It'd be okay for awhile, until I saw he would never talk to me."

"And then what would happen?"

"There would be no way out . . . I'd just be there."

"Do you believe that?"

"I knew you were going to ask me that. I guess, if I wanted, I could find a way. After all, I did it last week. But it seems so hard."

"Why?"

He sighed, dipped his head, and spoke in a strained voice. "You really want to know? It's hard because I'm not used to saying what I really feel to people."

"Why does that make it hard?"

178

"Because I never know what they're going to do. That's really it. I guess I've always dreaded them walking away or hitting me, like my father did." He furrowed his eyebrows. "But that wasn't so bad. It's really worth it." Sam smiled at me. "You know, we seem to talk about everything but my mother."

"Do you think so?"

"I don't know why I said that. I thought I'd be crying a lot, but I'm not. I don't want my mother to die. But if that's going to happen, maybe at least this can be a special time." He wiped his eyes. "You know, I've got this thing about a special time."

"Why the tears, Sammy?"

"I'm not unhappy. It's a new feeling for me. It's like saying, hey, Sammy, what you want is okay. So do it, trust yourself. Face the questions and see what you say. That's what, I guess, I've been doing here. Asking me—not my father, not a teacher, not you . . . just me."

"And how do you feel about that?"

"Like I just found a new person. Me. The kid who really cares about his mother and father."

Sam reached his hand out to me. When I clasped it firmly, he smiled. "Thanks," he whispered.

"Thank yourself," I said.

We both laughed and ended the session with a robust hug.

ᘓᘓ ᘓᘓ ᘓᘓ ᘓᘓ ᘓᘓ ᘓᘓ ᘓᘓ ᘓᘓ ᘓᘓ ᘓᘓ ᘓᘓ ᘓᘓ ᘓᘓ

Taking the steps three at a time, Sam sprinted up the stairs, his books barely contained in the backpack strapped to his shoulders. The chattering television bombarded him when he reached the second-floor landing. He walked directly into his mother's bedroom without his ritualistic hesitation.

Margaret Millen's head hung forward, dangling in front of her chest at such a sharp angle that it appeared disconnected from her body. A thick, green bathrobe bunched up in front of her chest. Another half-eaten meal decorated the hospital tray.

Sam's smile, a carefully rehearsed and orchestrated greeting, dissipated as he lingered near the bureau. Was something different? With each passing second, his stomach tightened like a vise, the blood crashing through his arteries as his heart rate accelerated rapidly. His mother's hands were stiff and still. No movements. He focused on her chest, fixating on every fold in the robe; waiting, praying for the material to move, quiver . . . anything. It couldn't be, a voice screamed within him. What about that special time? He started to approach her, fighting the numbness which spread from his fingers to his hands. Then he stopped, as if confronted by a physical barrier. Slowly, in nervous little steps, he backed out of the room into the hall. His vision blurred. Placing one foot in front of the other carefully, he moved down the staircase. He took each step as if he had been sleepwalking. His feet moved like lead weights. He used the railing in a manner similar to the way his mother used a cane. Suddenly, he stopped. A sharp, distinct cough filled his ears. Spinning around, he charged back up the stairs, jumped the last four steps, and leaped into the bedroom.

Startled by his frenzy, Margaret looked at him wide-eyed. He stared at her, smiling so broadly he thought his face would crack. They both laughed, but for very different reasons.

"I'm flattered," she said. "I never saw you in such a hurry to see me."

He nodded his head up and down, speechless.

"Well, are you going to move from that spot and kiss me?" she asked. Sam obeyed immediately. "That's better." She turned her face away from him to cough. The hacking spasms in her throat dominated her, forcing her to hunch over and hold her ribs until it passed. When she looked up again, her eyes were glazed and bloodshot.

"Do you want some water or juice, something for your throat?" Sam asked.

In a raspy, hoarse voice, she indicated the juice. He filled the glass and gave it to her. He could hear her teeth rattling against the glazed rim.

"How's school?" she asked.

"Would you mind if I didn't answer that question?" he said.

"It's okay, Sammy, I don't want to pry."

"Oh, no, Mom, you're not prying. I love when you ask me questions . . . just not that one. That one's such bull. I mean, who cares?"

"I do," Margaret said to her son. "I want to know what you're doing. There's not much else I can really experience from this bed. But, if you don't want to talk, it's okay. Want to play cards?"

"Ma, that's just it. Today, I'd like to talk."

"I don't understand. I thought you just said you—"

"I mean," he interrupted, "I didn't want to talk about that kind of stuff. I wanted to talk about you." He frowned and looked away.

"You don't have to get upset about me; I'm fine," she countered. "I feel better each day."

Uncomfortable, feeling he had trespassed, Sam nodded. "Let me empty this," he said, picking up the bedpan. For perhaps the hundredth time, he dumped its contents in the toilet, then rinsed it in the tub. He completed the chore quickly, but remained in the bathroom, leaning against the window, mumbling about the words he found so difficult to use. He grabbed the pan and returned to the bedroom, unaware that for the first time, he was neither dizzy nor nauseous.

The whine of the TV tuner, jumping from station to station, filled the room in direct response to the gadget in his mother's hand.

"Hey, you want to play cards?" Sam asked.

Clicking off the set, she nodded. Margaret rubbed the back of her neck with her hands, displaying considerable discomfort.

"Let me do that," Sam insisted. "The guys sometimes do it to each other before a track meet—it kind of loosens us up." He kneaded the muscles around her shoulder blades, then massaged her neck with a professional flair.

"That's great. Your hands are like a man's. They're strong, like your father's."

"Ma?"

"Yes, Sammy."

"How does it feel being so sick?" he said, trying to keep his voice steady. He could feel the muscles in her neck tense.

"Oh, you get used to it."

"But how does it feel?"

"Not as good as your hands on my neck. You can stop now," she counseled, "it feels much better."

"No, I'll do some more," he said, not wanting to face her. He felt freer to ask the questions when their eyes did not meet.

"Well?"

"Well, what?" Margaret asked.

"How does it feel?"

"The pain is the easiest part. Not being able to get around

like I used to, well, that's more difficult for me to handle. There's so many things I'd like to do for you and Daddy and Lisa; for Eddie and the other kids at St. Dominick's. You get to feel a little bit useless."

"We're doing just fine, Ma, I swear."

"Oh, I know you're taking care of yourself. But you should have a mother who can be with you—oh, you know, play tennis with, go to a restaurant, make your favorite dessert . . . meet your teacher at, at school." Margaret began to cry.

"Ma, it's okay, really it is. None of that matters. It used to, but it doesn't matter any more. Honest!" He held his hands tightly on her shoulders.

"I'm sorry," she whispered. "You shouldn't see me like this."

"But I want to help," he said, now willing to sit on the bed in front of her and look directly into her eyes. It was she who now avoided him. "Remember when I was in the hospital a long time ago." She nodded. "Well," he continued, "the best day of my life happened then. I was so darn scared and alone until you came and sat down on the bed. I didn't know what was happening. And you know what you did?" Margaret smiled through her tears, envisioning a scene which had taken place eight years before. "You asked me what I was frightened about and then you just explained everything about what was going on. It made such a difference that you just really talked to me honest. I'll never forget that. Never. So," he said, sighing rather noisily, "what I thought is, maybe, well . . . maybe now I could sit here and talk to you. You know. About how I feel and you feel and what we both think. That kind of stuff."

"I think I'd like that," she asserted. "Before, when you asked me what it feels like, there's one thing I didn't tell you. It can get very lonely being sick because everyone's afraid of talking about it. Even the person who's sick . . ." Her voice cracked as she struggled to continue. "Except if they're lucky enough to have a son like you."

"You're not mad, then?"

"No, Sammy, I'm not mad." She stroked his arm affectionately.

"Do you ever think about . . . about . . ." He paused, unable to say the word.

Margaret smiled at her son. "Do I ever think about dying? Is that what you wanted to ask me?" He bowed his head, undecided, unsure, until she lifted his chin. "Do you want to continue this?"

"Ma, I've been wanting to really talk like this to you for a whole year."

"Okay," she said. "Then let's do it. There's so many things I'd like to tell you too." Margaret took her son's hand and peered directly into his eyes. He smiled, then laughed. Margaret giggled like a little girl.

As the two of them began to share their thoughts, their fears and their love, Chad Millen arrived home. He set his attaché case on the table beside Sam's books. He picked up one of the texts and flipped through it casually. The lines on his face had deepened. As he began to climb the staircase, he became aware of voices in the bedroom. He slowed his pace.

"My mother never died on me," he heard Margaret say. "She just sort of disappeared little by little. What scares me, Sammy, is that you'll always remember me sick . . . the way I am now."

Chad's eyebrows furrowed, reflecting his instant rage. He knew Sammy had defied his edict. Although his first impulse was to charge into the bedroom and attack his son physically for betraying him, something deep inside stopped him as he overheard Sam's response to his wife's comment.

"I was afraid I'd only remember what's happening now, too," he replied to his mother, " 'cause I guess I never paid much attention, you know, to us, to our family. It was always there, permanent, like . . . like the Statue of Liberty." He paused. "I guess what I'm saying is that I never appreciated all of this until you got . . . got sick."

The anger that had surged within Chad dissipated. He sat on the steps and listened.

184

"I'm not sure that's really altogether true," Margaret countered, no longer relying on the pillows for support as she held her body upright and gestured with her hands. Though the darkness under her eyes and the gaunt cavities in her cheeks remained, a sudden animation accented the features of her face. "When you were eight . . . God, that seems like yesterday! Well, you came to me with a shoebox filled with all kinds of pretty rocks you found in the street. Do you remember?"

Sam nodded his head and shrugged his shoulders simultaneously. "A little . . . yeah."

"Well," she continued, "on that box, you printed in big funny letters a message I never forgot—'To The Best Mommy In The Whole Wide World.' I sure felt loved and appreciated, Sammy . . . just like I do right now."

Chad, too, remembered Sammy's little gift of rocks. The tears competed with the smile blossoming on his face. Give them more time, he told himself. For the next hour, he remained on the stairs and listened to his wife and son talk. Chad could no longer remember what he believed had been so important about camouflaging the truth. Words and images that he had dismissed previously as sentimental suddenly had a profound effect on him.

Inside the bedroom, Sam shifted positions several times, sensing he wanted more and more contact with his mother. He squatted on the bed directly in front of her and held both her hands. Margaret, visibly more lively, shook his hand often to accent her points. She grinned, knowing that she approached the punch line in her next story.

"So he said, 'Maggie, you stay right here,' and then he ran back to the car." Margaret held her hand over her mouth and raised her eyebrows. "Would you believe that your father came to propose and forgot the ring?"

They both laughed. Margaret became giddy, causing her son to howl at her antics. He never remembered feeling so free. Suddenly, Sam became aware of a figure looming in the doorway. He stopped laughing immediately.

Chad stood very erect; his hand gripping the molding like

185

some resurrected god. Despite the tension in his body, he smiled warmly at his son. When Sam sighed his relief, his father entered the room hesitantly.

Margaret watched her husband approach her. At first, she didn't understand the peculiar expression on his face. No one seemed to know how to begin. Finally, Chad said, "I'd like . . ." His voice faded. "Um, I'd . . ." The tears began to flow again. "I'd like to join . . . your, uh, conversation. I don't know if I'd be as good at it as you guys are . . . but, I'd, well, I'd like to try."

Margaret gestured for her husband to sit beside her. Chad embraced her and nodded, then eyed his son. In an uncharacteristic move, he kissed Sam on the cheek and hugged him. Margaret closed her eyes as she touched both of them. The muscles in her face relaxed into a very soft and very peaceful smile.

The old Fiat sputtered to a spastic stop in front of the Millen house. Lisa jumped out and released the catches which secured the canvas convertible top to the front windshield. She struggled against the accordion braces, finally lowering the unit. A large painting, draped in a blanket, loomed from the back seat. Lisa maneuvered the canvas over the door, rather than through it; an arduous feat owing to the substantial size of the painting relative to the diminutive size of the car. Finally, it was freed. A slight smile anointed her face. She peered under the blanket at the portrait, further punctuating her pleased expression. She could really say she liked it, in spite of Jessie's opinion.

When Lisa turned, she eyed the front of the house in which she had spent her first eighteen years. The slate roof, the louvered shutters, the columned porch, even the small weather vane which the original builder had fixed permanently to the chimney, remained exactly in place as if time could not erode even the smallest details of the structure. In six hundred years, she thought, this brick building might still be standing. Despite the down payment, the mortgage, and the furniture filling the interior, the occupants had only a temporary lease. It's a cha-

186

rade that confused her. The people who lived here, much like herself and her family, would appear and disappear with alarming regularity. And each family, like her own, would believe in the springtime and summer of their lives, rarely giving any serious recognition to the coming autumn and final winter.

It all seemed so permanent. For a moment, she hated the brick and the mortar. The exterior had lied to her. Inside, behind the front door, everything had changed. That's why outsides aren't important, she affirmed. You could fool people with the surface veneer . . . like she had done for so long, even to herself. For the first time, Lisa Millen wanted to be on the inside, even with its risks and momentary glow.

Picking up the painting with special care, she marched quickly up the steps. Rather than bring her gift to the door, Lisa deposited the painting at the bottom of the stairs so that her mother couldn't spot it on the console. She rang the doorbell and said "hi" into the monitor. Instead of the usual greeting from her mother through the speaker, Chad opened the door and smiled. "Hey, didn't expect you so early."

"I wanted more time with Mom . . . besides," she whispered, pointing to the painting, "I've got something for her." Lisa planted a compulsory kiss on her father's cheek and, for the first time, Chad knew it.

When Lisa reached for the painting, he said, "Wait. I'll help, honey."

Lisa stopped dead in her tracks and stared at her father with a look of puzzlement. He smiled at her. After breaking the gaze, they brought the portrait inside and rested it in the foyer.

Chad eyed it curiously. "May I?" he asked, holding the corner of the blanket in readiness.

"Oh . . . okay," she responded.

Together, they lifted the blanket, revealing the lifelike portrait of Maggie. Lisa split her attention between her father and the canvas.

Chad, straight-faced, nodded his head up and down without speaking. Relaxing his expression, he turned to his daughter.

"It's wonderful," he declared.

Lisa's mouth dropped open in amazement. In some way, she felt like she was five years old again. "Ya really think so?"

Chad's head bounced up and down affirming his "yes" response. His arm extended spontaneously and he touched Lisa's shoulder gently. They shared a quick, awkward smile, then grabbed the sides of the painting and began to climb the stairs. Three steps up, Chad paused, signaling Lisa to stop. He cleared his throat.

"Maybe one day," he began, "if you want someone to sit for a portrait, you'd, uh, think of me."

Lisa wanted to hug her father, but, somehow, couldn't get her arms to obey. "Sure, Dad," she beamed, "I'd love that."

They continued their ascent in silence. Upon entering the bedroom, they found Margaret asleep, her head to one side, and a family photo resting on her chest. They smiled and placed the still-covered surprise on top of the bureau facing the bed.

As soon as it was in place, as if on cue, Margaret opened her eyes.

"Hi, Mom," Lisa said softly. "Did we wake you?"

"It really doesn't matter, honey. As a woman of leisure, I have the prerogative to sleep any time I want."

"Notice anything different in the room, Mag?" Chad asked.

Maggie jested a casual, "Nope. There's the same old bureau, the same ol' thing on the bureau covered with a blanket . . . nothing new!"

Lisa giggled. "What do you say we disrobe 'the same old thing on the bureau,' for you?"

Chad and Lisa stood in readiness at both ends of the painting.

With a sudden gust of energy, Maggie called, "Hurry up and get that thing off. I can't wait another second."

Chad and Lisa looked at each other and with a nod of Lisa's head, whipped the blanket off.

The portrait startled Margaret. She gasped, putting her hands over her mouth and staring at the image. Almost a minute passed without any of them talking. Finally, Maggie extended

188

her hand toward her daughter. Lisa touched her mother's frail fingers, then hugged her.

"Well, ladies, that's the cue for my exit," Chad interjected. He kissed both his wife and daughter, then left the room.

"Here I am," Maggie whispered, "sick and achy and feeling that I'm the luckiest person in the world." She paused. "By the way, who's that lady in the picture?"

Lisa laughed. She had almost forgotten her mother's natural humor.

The two women spent almost fifteen minutes admiring the portrait. Lisa talked about Jessica's analysis of the painting and, to her surprise, Margaret loved the concept of a combined image with pieces of both herself and her daughter embodied in a single face.

"You know, you look great, Mom," Lisa volunteered. "Better than I've seen you in weeks."

Margaret acknowledged the comment silently, still engrossed in the painting. "That's the way I'd like to be remembered," she said in a barely audible voice.

"C'mon," Lisa interjected, "stop that kind of talk."

Margaret closed her eyes. "I'm not being morbid . . . really!" A pause. "Lisa, do you want to talk?"

The quality of her mother's question was oddly familiar. "You've been speaking with Sam too, haven't you?"

Margaret nodded. They both laughed.

"Well, here goes," Lisa said, avoiding eye contact with her mother. "There's something I've never told you about."

"And there's things I've never told you about," Margaret countered.

They peered into each other's eyes. During the next three hours, Lisa and her mother shared more freely than they had at any other time in their lives . . . going beyond the veneer, beyond the brick and mortar.

A bright stream of light filtered through the windows and bathed Margaret in hues of yellow and orange as she sat comfortably in the recliner sipping tea. Her hair had been combed neatly away from her face. She wore a dressier bathrobe than usual. During the past six weeks, since the open conversation with Sam, Margaret began to demonstrate more strength and resiliency despite the seemingly irreversible nature of her illness. The roundtable discussions, as Chad nicknamed them, became a nightly tradition. Nothing had been left unsaid. Each day had become a cause for active celebration; Margaret Millen had remained among them.

On two separate occasions, Chad, with Sam's help, arranged to transport Eddie from St. Dominick's to their home. They carried him, atop his wheelchair, up the long flight of stairs into the bedroom, leaving him with Maggie for their infamous card games. She traded teaching time for each of her victories, a bargain which helped her teach Eddie how to hold a pencil and make simple lines on sheets of paper.

Margaret leaned back in the chair and watched her husband admiringly as he dressed for work. Chad fixed his tie and adjusted the collar of his suit jacket.

Aware of his wife's gaze, he said, "You know, you're looking better today, my lady . . . and that's a straightforward, serious assessment."

"Must be the sunlight blinding your vision—my man," she quipped playfully, then grinned. "I am feeling better today." Suddenly, Sam darted into the room with a stack of books under one arm. "Gonna miss my bus," he blurted. He kissed his mother and paused for a moment. He, too, noticed the energy in her expression. "Hey, you look good, Ma." Sam winked at her, patted his father's shoulder, and exited quickly. "See you later," he hollered from the hallway.

"Take care," Margaret said loudly.

"Don't worry, I will."

Several seconds later, the front door slammed shut. Margaret nodded her head. "Chad, I think I'll finish my tea sitting at the window, if you wouldn't mind moving me over there."

As Chad pushed the chair, Margaret concentrated on holding her cup steady. "We made it," she cheered after he positioned her directly in front of the window.

"How's that?" he asked, sitting down on the arm of the recliner and trying to survey the scene from her viewpoint.

"Perfect!" She lifted her head slowly. "Look at that special sky, Chad." Low, white puffy clouds, hovered in a bright, blue sky. "This must be my lucky day."

Ten minutes later, Margaret Millen, aged thirty-nine, left her body. A soft smile remained on the frozen features of her face.

ABOUT THE AUTHORS

Barry Neil Kaufman and Suzi Lyte Kaufman, both born and raised in New York City, teach a uniquely loving lifestyle and vision called the Option Process, which has both educational and therapeutic applications. They are mentors and teachers to individuals and groups (The Option Institute and Fellowship, R.D. #1, Box 174A, Sheffield, Mass. 01257) and lecture in universites, hospitals, and have appeared often in mass media throughout the country.

As a result of their innovative and successful "Option" program for their once-autistic child and other developmentally delayed or brain-imparied children, the Kaufmans also counsel and instruct families wanting to create home-based teaching environments for their own special children. They also teach professionals in this area.

Mr. Kaufman has written seven books, coauthored two screenplays with his wife (winning the coveted Christopher Award twice and also the Humanitas Award), and has had articles featured in major publications. His first book, "Son-Rise," which details his family's inspiring journey with their once-autistic child, was dramatized as an NBC-TV special network presentation. "To Love Is To Be Happy With" shares the specific application of their nonjudgmental living and learning process as it applies to different life situations. In "Giant Steps," Barry Neil Kaufman gives us very caring, intimate, and uplifting portraits of young people he has worked with and touched during times of extreme crisis. "A Miracle To Believe In" recounts the emotional and oftentimes miraculous story of the Kaufmans' teaching another family and a group of volunteers to love themselves and, in turn, to love a little Mexican boy back to life in defiance of all the medical professionals who turn their backs after labeling the little boy's case hopeless. "A Land Beyond Tears" (co-authored with his wife) presents a liberating approach to death and dying. His latest book, "A Sense of Warning," shares the stranger-than-fiction, life-changing psychic experiences that led the Kaufmans to their current work and teaching.

Currently, in addition to working with others, Bears (as he is called) and Suzi Kaufman are at work on two new books, one fiction and one nonfiction, both of which have their seeds in the Option experience.